CASS LIBRARY OF AFRICAN STUDIES

GENERAL STUDIES

No. 121

Editorial Adviser: JOHN RALPH WILLIS
Department of History, University of California, Berkeley

A HISTORY

OF

THE BEJA TRIBES OF THE SUDAN

A HISTORY

OF

THE BEJA TRIBES

OF THE SUDAN

BY

A. PAUL

With corrections by the author

FRANK CASS & CO. LTD.

Published by
FRANK CASS AND COMPANY LIMITED
67 Great Russell Street, London WC1B 3BT
Reprinted by permission of the Cambridge University Press

Distributed in the United States by
International Scholarly Book Services, Inc.
Beaverton, Oregon 97005

Library of Congress Catalog Card No. 79–171836

ISBN 0 7146 1710 5

First edition   1954
New impression   1971

Printed in Great Britain by
Stephen Austin and Sons Ltd., Hertford.

ERRATA

(added by the author)

Page 5   *Footnote:* Besharn in place of Besharin.

Page 28   Lines 32–34: It is now known that Turin papyrus is not a representation of the Derheib mine, but of the quarries in the Wadi Hammat.

Page 58   *Footnote:* Vospicius in place of Vospicus.

Page 61   Line 15: The word "to", immediately before (Primis) should be omitted. The line should read, "I fought with the Blemmyes from Ibrim (Primis) to Talmis."

Page 77   Pedigree: The top arrow should come above the = below, and not over the word Hadat.

Page 79   The second brackets should be omitted.

Page 95   Pedigree: No. 5 of Gwilai's wives should read: ? (Nabtabia / Beni Amria).

CONTENTS

LIST OF PLATES

LIST OF MAPS

PREFACE

My purpose has been to present in as complete and consecutive form as possible the history of the tribes which now inhabit the mountains and deserts of the Eastern Sudan. It has not been an easy task nor, in the midst of official duties, have I been able to devote to it as much time as I should have liked. The student of Beja history must, moreover, be a master of tongues, ancient and modern, to an extent to which I cannot pretend.

I have been sparing of my notes, not wishing to distract the reader with over-abundance of often not very rewarding references, but the bibliography given at the end omits, I hope, no works which have useful reference to the Beja.

My acknowledgements are due to all those who have helped me with information and advice, more particularly to the Librarian of the Newbold Library in the University College of Khartoum, who most courteously allowed me to borrow as many books as I liked, to the Commissioner for Archaeology, who permitted me to read the manuscript notes of the late Sir Douglas Newbold (now in the Ashmolean Museum, Oxford) which I found invaluable, and to Mohammed Saleh Effendi Dirar Ali Yangi of the Eastern Telegraph Co., Port Sudan, whose encyclopedic knowledge of the tribes of the Red Sea coast was placed freely at my disposal.

I must also express my gratitude to the Sudan Government and to the Syndics of the University Press, Cambridge, for generous assistance in the publication of this book.

A. P.

Kassala, 1954

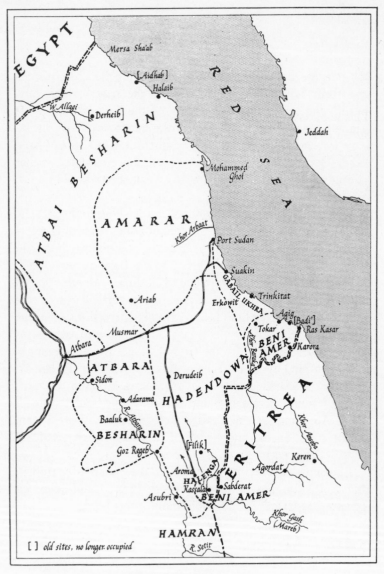

Map 1. The Beja Country

CHAPTER I

INTRODUCTION

A great and haughty nation, proud in arms.   MILTON

This volume is an attempt to trace the history of a people of the
Sudan of truly ancient stock, the Bugiha of Leo Africanus, the
Bugiens of seventeenth-century cartographers, the Blemmyes
of Roman times, the Bugas of the Axumite inscriptions, who
were quite possibly also the Buka of the Egyptian hieroglyphs,
and who, since medieval times, have been known to the world
as the Beja, and who for the forty centuries of their known
history have watched civilizations flourish and decay, and,
themselves almost unchanging, have survived them all. There
will be those who, when the tale is told, will question whether
the effort involved might not have been directed to ends more
profitable. Beja records are indeed scanty. There are periods,
whole centuries long, which for the chronicler are all but void,
and even when all that is known is marshalled and sifted, there
is much which must remain problematical and conjectural.
There will be those also who may accuse me of unwarrantable
deductions and suppositions unsupported by evidence. To this
I can but reply that I have deduced nothing inherently improbable, either from known facts, or from what I know of the
Beja today; and in this attempt to recall from obscurity the past
of a most fascinating race I am prepared, like Barth 'to contend
against the strong prejudices of numerous critics who are
accustomed to refuse belief to whatever is incapable of bearing
the strictest enquiry'.[1]

Moreover (or this book had never been written) there appears
to me to be much that is worthy of study in the evolution of
a race which knew Pharaoh in splendour and decline, which
fought not unsuccessfully against Rome, which has withstood
invasion and infiltration from the earliest times until the most

[1] *Travels*, vol. II (London, 1857), p. 253.

I

recent with the utmost resilience, and which today, if it accepts the 'Pax Britannica', does so with reservations and with frequent reversions to ancient ways, which are certainly not those of peace.

Properly to understand the Beja [wrote one who knew them well] we must delve into history, and in doing so we cannot fail to be struck by the pertinacity and vigour of a race which has attracted the attentions, welcome and unwelcome, and felt the impact of more powerful nations from time immemorial without experiencing any real disintegration or loss of morale.[1]

As a record of survival it is indeed unique, attributable partly to the inhospitality of the country in which they live, but more particularly to definite traits of character, preserved almost intact by their free, nomadic way of life; to an extraordinary mental and physical toughness, and no moral over-sensitiveness. The mental toughness is reflected in an obtuse and almost hostile reserve, in a determination to survive, long bred in them by the harshnesses of their life and environment, by the blood-feuds which are still their accepted custom, and by the tribal wars which have long been their relaxation. Among the Beja little value is set upon the sanctity of human life, a callous trait common to most primitive peoples, but by them shared particularly with other warrior Hamitic peoples, the Shilluk of the Upper Nile, and the Masai of the Tanganyika plains. Rude, wild, bestial, call them what you will, of unpleasant and unhygienic habits, their hair clotted with mutton fat, their bodies reeking of oil, sweat and woodsmoke, the Beja, for those whose knowledge of them goes beyond externals, will ever be a fascinating and rewarding study.

Throughout their long history they have remained supreme individualists, unamenable to authority, living widely dispersed and solitary among their deserts and mountain glens, impervious to external contacts, preserving, as though by their very

[1] D. Newbold, 'The Beja Tribes of the Red Sea Hills', in *The Anglo-Egyptian Sudan from Within*, ed. Hamilton (1935), p. 144.

aloofness and lack of curiosity, their freedom, their virility and their individuality. Wanting nothing of the world, they ask nothing better than that it should ask nothing of them. So it is they have rejoiced always in periods of weak government, or better still, of none at all, in which they are left to themselves to graze their herds, prosecute their feuds, and harry their neighbours as the spirit moves them.

The superficial portrait thus presented, that of a primitive and bloodthirsty desert tough, is admittedly an unattractive one, and could be supplemented and adorned by excerpts from the chronicles of all those whose lot has fallen among them from the earliest times. To the dynastic Egyptians they were the 'hateful Kush'. Pomponius Mela in the second century A.D. records that they are 'scarcely human but rather like wild beasts'. A thousand years later the Arab writer, Ibn Jubayr, says of them that they 'live like animals. This is the country of Islam which more than any other deserves extermination.' Juan de Castro, who took part in the unsuccessful Portuguese expedition against Suez in 1540, relates that they 'were given to stealth and rapine above all other people'.[1] Linant de Bellefonds, the French engineer who visited the Southern Atbai in 1833, thought rather better of them, though admitting their faults in full: 'liars to excess, thieves when the occasion offers, lazy beyond all description, yet brave, loyal, and often chivalrous'.[2] The German Schweinfurth, visiting roughly the same area in 1864, is less favourable: 'inhospitable without exception, false and secretive. . . as repellent as the thorns and as clinging as the prickles of their native plants.'[3] Abel Chapman, a naturalist, who visited the northern Hadendowa in 1921, thought them 'the most sullen and incompetent of savages',[4] and writer after writer has no better, and even worse, to say of them.

To their neighbours, whether Roman Egypt, or the Nuba,

[1] Kennedy Cooke, 'The Red Sea Coast in 1540', *Sudan Notes and Records*, vol. XVI (2) (1933), p. 159.
[2] *L'Etbaye* (1884), p. 130. [3] From a translation in the Newbold MS.
[4] From the Newbold MS.

and later the Arabs, of the Nile valley, the Beja have appeared always as an inimical and ferocious people, liberally endowed with most devilish characteristics, which may account for the story current among Arab chroniclers in the Sudan that they are descendants of a Ginn named Hafhaf, or Sakhr, who deceived King Solomon (Sulieman ibn Daud) in the matter of one of his wives. But in a record such as this, of a primitive survival in a world becoming progressively more complex, it is unreasonable to look for the refinements to which we ourselves are now accustomed, nor should we forget that our ancestors must have appeared very similar to the Roman invaders of our shores in 54 B.C., brutal, uncouth, and inimical to strangers. In the two thousand years which have elapsed since then we have become an altogether different people: not so the Beja, who remain now much as we and they were then, a primitive, warlike and untamable race of savages.

It is, moreover, only in the course of the last fifty years, or even less, that they have been subjected, for the first time in their history, to any real attempt at orderly administration which aims at achieving all that is to be gained from security, elimination of disease and famine, education, and development of their sparse natural resources. The effect upon a people so impervious to change has scarcely had time to show itself: yet they are perhaps now less prone than once to resort to the sword as the arbiter of all disputes, and rather more ready to maintain their rights by negotiation, which for them is a process of the most audacious advocacy, endless compromise, and masterly and repeated procrastination. This gift for compromise I believe to be one of the most deep-seated of all Beja characteristics, but it is only in recent years and under peaceful conditions that it has had opportunity to expand and develop, and to be applied to 'lesser breeds without the law'. Their capacity for litigation is immense. No case, especially one involving rights of land or water, ever ends, and they will come together and spend days in apparently endless discussion of the most minute differences with all the vigour, time-wasting

4

sophistries, irrelevant evasions, and unmannerly vituperation of medieval scholastics; yet in the last resort '*Sharia* law, as interpreted by uneducated but honest tribal Kadis, is the canon applied to all cases which cannot be settled by the more gentlemanly method of give-and-take tribal compromise'.[1]

In other ways also the Beja are showing signs of greater amenability and good-neighbourliness, all of which must be accounted as gain to those responsible for their administration in a race so utterly conservative and self-sufficient, which in the past has had every reason to be distrustful of strangers and for which a mere half-century is all too short a time in which to alter innate prejudices and age-long beliefs. And though their ultimate savageness is yet only partly tamed, they happily retain the greater part of their primitive virtues: simplicity, fortitude and patience; fearlessness and generosity; a broad and far from infrequent sense of humour; and latterly, to those who have won their confidence, they have given loyalty and affection. Such confidence is not easily bestowed, and is all the more to be valued for that very reason. 'Anyone', said a one-time Beja district commissioner, 'can tame a dog; when a wolf is responsive it warms the heart.'

The qualities which today more than any others impress the observer are their aloofness, their indolence and absorbtion in their own affairs, allied to a most rigid and uncompromising regard for the integrity of territory and tribal rights. The ground under their feet, upon which they graze their animals, or grow their scanty crops, is to them sacrosanct and inalienable, to be surrendered only to superior force, though by development of their instinct for compromise they do not object to usufruct by favoured interlopers so long as the title is not in dispute. They are unusually tenacious of their rights of ownership, and equally ready to use force in their defence. The Hadendowa, certainly the most openly aggressive of the Beja tribes, regard the preservation (and, be it said, the expansion) of their territory as of such importance that they have placed on certain sections

[1] Sandars, 'The Besharn', *S.N.R.* vol. XVI (2) (1933), p. 144.

the particular duty of its defence against encroachment by other tribes. Thus on the east the Gemilab maintain the frontier against their traditional foes the Beni Amer, the Besharin on the west are kept at bay by the Shaboidinab, and the Mahmou-dalihadab, a small section on the Atbara, are responsible for preventing trespass by the Shukria.

This attitude of the Beja towards their tribal territory is perhaps best illustrated by their reaction to the threat of Italian invasion of the Sudan in the summer and autumn of 1940. When the Italians occupied Kassala there were fears that the Beja might get out of hand, or even materially assist the enemy, and indeed, in the obvious state of our unpreparedness, they might well have been excused for believing a British defeat inevitable. That the Beja, and the Hadendowa in particular, at all times rendered the most valuable services without apparent thought for the consequences of an Italian victory, became a matter of some self-congratulation to their administrators, being re-garded as evidence of the rightness of our methods, and the popularity of our rule. I have my doubts. While admitting that loyalty in some measure inspired their efforts I am almost certain, from what I know of the Beja character, that they viewed the war with very different eyes to ours. The Italians employed in their colonial armies large numbers of Tigré-speaking troops, many of them Beni Amer and cognate tribes, and with these, the ancient enemies of the Hadendowa, they threatened invasion from Khor Baraka to the river Atbara. This was something which could by no means be allowed, and the war in which they so wholeheartedly supported us was for the Hadendowa but another incident, albeit a major one, in an ancient feud. It was a war fought in defence of tribal territory, and that the British had approximately similar objectives in their efforts to defeat the Italians was merely incidental. When it was all over they were extremely annoyed to find themselves de-prived of the fruits of victory, which for them meant unlimited loot of Beni Amer cattle, and a general and enjoyable harrying of the tribe as a whole.

INTRODUCTION

Of Beja indolence it is almost superfluous to speak. No
nomad is fond of hard work, even in the service of his precious
herds, but in this the Beja far surpass anything within my experience. Leisure is more to them almost than life: of manual
labour they will none, and they will starve rather than set their
hand to tasks which with a little effort would ensure a certain
degree of prosperity and freedom from want. It is true that the
Amarar now provide much of the dock labour at Port Sudan,
but for the cultivation of their cotton holdings in Tokar and
the Gash Delta the Beja rely on West African and Eritrean
labour, their interest in the matter being confined to the collection of the benefits of the industry of others on pay-day, and
in encouraging their animals to trespass on the cultivation when
no one is looking. Even in the herding of their animals they
will often employ the otherwise despised Tigré who, though
themselves Beja of a very ancient stock, have been schooled by
long ages of serfdom to labour for others for little reward.

The Beja today probably eat far more grain than did their
milk-drinking ancestors, but they grow little of it themselves,
even when opportunity offers, though under certain circumstances they are not averse to indulging in husbandry of a sort,
if so it can be called:

When some fortunate rain falls and the *khors* spate from the hills
the tribesman scatters a little seed, and without cleaning or fencing
his plot hopes three months later to return and harvest the fruit of
his labours. Stray camels...find and devour this unexpected suc-
culence, to the high indignation of its owner who then considers
himself entitled to preposterously exaggerated compensation.[1]

The essence of the whole operation, as in the growing of
cotton, is that no work is involved, and that the reward is enjoyable only when it can be obtained with a minimum of exer-
tion, or better still, none at all. They have been unwilling even
to make the most of their main asset, their livestock. They

[1] Clark, 'The Manners, Customs and Beliefs of the Northern Beja', *S.N.R.*
vol. XXI (1) (1938), p. 19.

breed an excellent strain of camel, and the southern sections have large herds of cattle, but apart from a few camels sold to the government as police remounts or in Egyptian markets they are utterly uninterested in the possibilities of the stock market, and have allowed the extremely profitable camel trade with Egypt to become the monopoly of the acute gypsy tribe of Rashaida, who are only recent immigrants from the Hedjaz. They are now less allergic than before to any sort of hard work, but they are at all times indifferent and erratic workers and with the money earned from an acre or two of cotton, or from a few weeks' labour on the Port Sudan quays, will retire to their hills the richer perhaps by a camel or a few goats, there to idle away their time until need or inclination drives them again to work.

Theirs is admittedly an inhospitable country whose very barrenness and lack of fertility emphasize the futility of effort, and this, allied to memories of a warrior past, when all essential tasks were done by slaves or captives, has helped to mould the Beja reaction to labour which may make demands upon their energy:

They sit in the exiguous shade of their prized acacias watching their attenuated herds at graze, and priding themselves that they are...overlords of countless leagues of country, exempted for ever from the degrading necessity of manual labour.[1]

It is an attitude which might spring from mere stupidity, were it not that the Beja are by no means a stupid race, nor even quite so uncouth or Boetian as they themselves very often give the impression, largely with the object of discouraging the tedious attentions and enquiries of strangers. There are some very acute though undeveloped minds to be found under the most unlikely mops of hair, and their language alone, rich, intricate and discursive, is not the tongue of a slow-witted or unimaginative people, and shows traces of an ordered and well-matured culture. They are great raconteurs, and both among the

---

[1] Clark, op. cit. p. 20.

To Bedawie- and Tigré-speaking tribes a well-stocked mind and a fluent tongue are in great demand during the hours of almost limitless idling beneath the shade trees of the well centres, or over the coffee cup round the camp fire of an evening.

Attention has been called not infrequently to their alleged stupidity as evidenced by a notable lack of scholastic success, despite over twenty years of intense effort by the government to make it otherwise. This has been attributed mainly to the initial difficulties experienced in learning the language of instruction, Arabic. This may be so to a certain extent, but I attribute it far more to a fundamental lack of interest, and the unreceptiveness of the Beja mind in dealing with things outside the sphere of their normal agelong pastoral environment. At the best they may only half absorb new ideas, and all but completely misunderstand them, and I am inclined to believe that they will never develop much further mentally until either their standard of living can be raised very considerably, as is happening in the Gash, or their primitive desert environment suffers a complete transformation, which to say the least is most unlikely.

Of their aloofness it is enough to say that they have had little or no cause throughout their long history to repose much confidence in strangers. All those who have gone to the Beja country since the earliest times have done so for the purposes of exploitation. The Pharaohs wanted gold, the Ptolemies gold and also elephants for their Asian campaigns. The Sabaeans and the later Himyarites came for trade and remained as a dominant aristocracy. The Romans were less rapacious; they wanted only marble and other similar stone for their monuments, and were otherwise content to let the Beja well alone. The Arab intruders of the Middle Ages came for gold and precious stones, and the Turco-Egyptians who succeeded them for loot of any description, setting an example as yet unsurpassed of senseless oppression, cruelty, and the plunder of all who were so unfortunate as to be within their power to dominate. The British, the last invaders with whom the Beja have had to deal, have indeed refrained from extortion and barbarity, yet it is perhaps not easy for the Beja to forget the battlefields in which they were mowed down by gunfire in support of the corrupt and decrepit Egyptians who had so misruled them. It is not surprising, therefore, that distrust of strangers is deeply ingrained in the Beja mind, and though now with the passing of the years they are prepared to admit our good intentions, we have a passion for orderly government of which they most heartily disapprove.

The Beja live in small family groups scattered here and there wherever some scant pasture or water is to be found, and even when discovered in the recesses of their hills and deserts the lack of a common language intrudes an all but insurmountable barrier to closer relationships.

A loosely coherent patriarchal society wandering in small groups over the plains in search of grass... which has evolved in the course of time a machinery for settling its own affairs, adapted to its environment and needs, based largely on the universal Beja axioms of procrastination and forbearance.[1]

The difficulty of their language, and their reluctance to speak any other, quite apart from their natural antipathy to strangers, makes the task of administration more than ordinarily difficult, and one which is by no means eased by the frequency with which political officers in the service of the Sudan Government are transferred from one district to another. District commissioners after two or three years spent in mastering the intricacies of the Beja tongue, and in getting to know the people in other ways, are no sooner in a position usefully to apply their hard-won knowledge than they are whisked away to attend to the administrative wants of the Fur or the Azande, and have to start all over again in an entirely different environment. However commendable such a policy may be with a view to giving the administrator as wide an experience as possible, and in preventing him from becoming too parochial, a more flexible policy

[1] Sandars, 'The Besharin', *S.N.R.* vol. XVI (2) (1933), p. 149.

which would have allowed those who showed aptitude for a particular form of administration to remain rather longer in their posts would have paid handsome dividends, and nowhere more so than among the Beja. Five or six years is not too long for a sympathetic administrator, who has learned the language, to bring his knowledge and experience to bear to the advantage of the government and the people whom he serves.

Few, however, have remained as long, and it is small wonder therefore that the Beja, with all their reserve, evasiveness and carefully cultivated obtuseness, entrenched behind the obscurities of their language, have been the despair of many of their administrators; yet there are few who have served among them who have left them without regret, and who in other times and places have not known a nostalgia for the bare clean-swept spaces of the Atbai, the high mountain valleys in the glory of their winter rains, and even for the dusty tamarisk-fringed labyrinths of the Baraka and the Gash, where strolling aloof and unconcerned among them all, may be found the unchanging 'Fuzzy' with his easy nomad stride and his 'hay-rick head of hair', his camel stick aslant across his shoulders, and an occasional goat, his familiar spirit, trotting dog-like at his heels.

CHAPTER II

THE BEJA COUNTRY AND ITS TRIBES

The gaunt and leopard coloured lands.   FREYA STARK

The Beja, although nearly all their tribes have acquaintance
with the sea, grazing their camels and cattle along its margins
for some' season of every year (some of them being even accustomed to drink sea water), are yet landsmen without exception. They have no aptitude with boats, and though some
of them must count the Fish-Eaters of classical times among
their remote ancestors, and though the sea along their coasts
abounds in fish, they look with contempt on the trade of fisher-
man, and only a few sections will eat fish, even in times of
severest want. Indeed, they regard the sea with abhorrence,
if only because by this means so many strangers have come to
their land and bothered them with their attentions. Nevertheless, for hundreds of miles, from Mersa Sha'ab on the Egyptian
frontier to Ras Kasar in the south, the sea is their eastern
boundary, bordered by a narrow strip of shelving plain from
which the hills lift their abrupt and serried ranges, falling away
gradually and imperceptibly to the distant reaches of the Nile
and Atbara across the wide hill-pocked plains of the Atbai, of
Odi and Tibilol. The whole area from Halaib to the Atbara is
in summer afflicted by intense heat and suffocating sandstorms,
so that even in the comparative cool of the high glens of Erkowit
the landscape may be obscured for days at a time, and in Tokar
dust-storms of unbelievable density and fury blow almost daily
from mid-June to September.

Such is the Beja country, some 110,000 square miles of coast,
mountain and plain, the greater part unfruitful desert and
barren waste of rock and sand, a country, except at brief
seasons of the year, intensely arid and inhospitable. Yet this
sparse country, where to exist at all seems scarcely possible,
carries an ever-increasing population of about 285,000 nomads,

subsisting for the most part on their herds of camels, cattle, goats and sheep, eked out in the northern deserts by occasional cultivation in a year of exceptional rains, and by sale of a few animals and a little charcoal in Egyptian markets such as Assuan on the river. The more southerly tribes are more fortunate. Earnings from labour in the docks at Port Sudan help to increase the standard of living among the Amarar, and nearly every tribe has a stake in the cotton schemes of Tokar and the Gash Delta. In the southern regions, too, the rainfall is heavier and less uncertain. Grazing is better, and in a good year the tribesman can grow sufficient grain to be self-supporting. But in the whole of this area there is evidence pointing to an extremely dry climate extending into the past for a period of some three to four thousand years. Conditions in historical times, therefore, have been much the same as they are today, though it is probable that the introduction of the camel and development of the charcoal industry have been responsible for further ecological depression within comparatively recent times. It is under these conditions that the Beja have endured and survived for four thousand years, and developed the art of existence.

North and inland of Port Sudan lie the hills and plains of the Atbai, refreshed only occasionally by a scanty summer rainfall, never perhaps more than two inches at its heaviest, and often nothing at all: a wild, inhospitable, and thinly populated country of sand and rocky outcrops, whose *wadis* afford scant grazing for goat and camel, ascending gradually from the Nile valley to the high mountain crests which overlook the narrow Red Sea plain. There on the coast conditions are not greatly different, save that the rain falls in winter and with greater regularity. The grazing can be excellent, and for this reason the narrow strip of the Gwineb, which lies between the hills and the sea from Halaib in the north to the fringes of the Tokar Delta in the south, is invaded every rainy season by a motley of Beja tribes in search of grazing for their animals, until such time as the grass dies back in March or early April, and they retreat once more to the landward plains or into the higher hills which, in this winter season especially, are the glory of the Beja country. Here among the high peaks of Erba, Asotriba and Elba, north of Port Sudan, are to be found mountain glens where there is running water, and relieving shade and ample grazing all the year round, 'rivers of water in a dry place, as the shadow of a great rock in a weary land'. The lesser ranges, below 4000 ft., are green and lush only for the short season of the winter rains, a mass of sharp, serrated ridges and of eroded and sun-tortured rock, stricken into the most fantastic shapes, which fall away sharply to the beds of the swift descending torrents which carry the winter floods down to the salt-encrusted fringes and islands of the Red Sea.

In these northern deserts man is the parasite of his herds, for whose subsistence he must be a wanderer ever in search of new pastures and grazing grounds. Their condition and health are vital to his own existence, and water and grass essentials without which they, and therefore he himself, may not long endure. Large-scale seasonal migrations such as take place in the west are unusual, except perhaps to the Gwineb in a year of good winter rains. The tendency is rather to split up into small groups, each of which, a single family or part of a family, seeks out a particular restricted area of pasturage which is all that the uncertain and extremely local rainfall affords. Migration on a large scale might easily end in disaster to man and beast. Under such conditions the family rather than the *badana* (still less the more recently created *hissa*) is the most important unit in tribal life, and the family heads thus wield considerable authority.

The configuration of the country in which they live lends itself to separation and isolation. In those wide arid spaces are to be found only occasional pockets of grazing, or some sparse vegetation in a narrow *khor*. Here and there the vagaries of the rainfall permit a little cultivation, and in and around such pockets as these, and the occasional isolated well centres, a few Beja families will be found living a life apart and intensely lonely, a life which serves always to intensify the individualism of the often tiny clans which wander about in their cycles within the

PLATE I

A VIEW OF THE RED SEA HILLS

orbit of the tribal whole. They are aloof even to members of their own tribe who do not live near them, and this aloofness tends to deepen into dislike when they meet the people of other races. In these wastes dwell the Um Ali and some of the Um Nagi Besharin, a remote and handsome race of nomads, but lightly administered, living always on the bare edge of existence, and breeding camels of the famous Ba Nagir and Kiliewau strain. Farther south, and living under conditions not greatly different, are the Amarar, a hardy, independent people, less nomadic than most, and less allergic to settled conditions and urban environment. They are probably of purer Beja stock than either the Hadendowa or Besharin, speak the most obscure and classic dialect of To Bedawie,[1] and have a reputation as formidable fighters whom no other tribe would care to meet on equal terms.

Immediately south of Port Sudan lie the hills and valleys of Sinkat and Erkowit, and south and west again the vast ranges of the Warriba massif, last refuge of Osman Digna, and still known only to a few of the wildest of the Hadendowa clans, sloping westwards to the plains of Odi and Tibilol, featureless, barren and dust-swept in winter, but beloved of the Hadendowa for the excellence of their grazing, their cool climate, and conditions healthy for both man and beast during the summer rains. The northern Hadendowa are hillmen, not greatly distinguishable in their mode of life from the Amarar or the Besharin. They are to be found scattered through the hills from Sinkat southwards towards Derudeib and Khor Baraka, where they join hands with their brethren of the south, a more numerous people centred on the Gash and the river Atbara, and for administrative purposes comprising the three Khuts of the Gash, Frontiers, and Atbara river, as against two, Northern and Odi, of the hill Hadendowa.

---

[1] According to Roper ('Poetry of the Hadendiwa', *S.N.R.* vol. x (1927), p. 147) there are five main dialects as spoken by the Hadendowa, Amarar, Besharin, Ababda and Halenga, the latter two having all but died out. As regards the Halenga I do not think that this is so. The Halenga were originally Tigré speakers, and some still are, but all without exception now speak To Bedawie as their mother tongue.

The Hadendowa today are the most numerous, probably the most powerful, certainly the most truculent of the Beja tribes, a tough and outwardly sullen people, who lack the charm which distinguishes so many of the Amarar and Besharin. They are remarkable also for being cattle- rather than camel-owners, and for their controlling interest in the cotton cultivations of the Gash Delta, south of which again lies the river Atbara where the Hadendowa and the Um Nagi/Besharin between them occupy the whole of the north-east bank between the Butana bridge and Sidon. The pools of the Atbara provide water all the year round, so that the Besharin have tended to become sedentary, and to cultivate its islands and verges. The Hadendowa, however, have remained nomadic, interested only in the riverain grazing, a subject of acrimonious dispute with the Shukria on the farther bank.

In and around Kassala are the Halenga, and still farther south on the north bank of the Setit there still survives the remnant of the once powerful tribe of the Hamran. Here the rainfall averages thirteen or fourteen inches per annum, and the grazing between Kassala and the Setit, utilized by the Rashaida and some of the Beni Amer, is excellent, but the tribes in this area have largely abandoned nomadism and have settled down to a sedentary existence.

The Gwineb, the great winter grazing area on the Red Sea coast, comes to an end where the Baraka debouches from the hills into the Tokar Delta, which like the Gash, has been developed for the cultivation of cotton, a profitable undertaking for the tribes whose administrative centre is the squalid mud-built town of Tokar situated in the middle of the Delta. These tribes, the Arteiga, Ashraf, Kimmeilab, Nurab, Shaiab, and Hassanab, known collectively as the *Gabail Ukhra* (Other Tribes) are not real Beja, though they have all lived among them since early medieval times, have intermarried with them, and have acquired their language and customs. Here also, sharing in the profits of the cotton crop and spending them prodigally, are a number of Hadendowa sections, some Beni Amer, and a few Amarar.

South of the Delta the physical features of the country change again: the mass of the hills grows denser and more solid, towering upwards to the 9000 ft. peak of Hamoyeit on the Sudan-Eritrean frontier, and the high plateau of Hagar Nush beyond. Here for the few months of the winter rains the hill country is unbelievably lovely. Grass grows luxuriantly in the upland valleys and meadows 'where blaze the unimaginable flowers', and mountain streams gush and sparkle with all the vivacity of a Highland river. From December onwards, if the rains be early enough, this nomad's paradise, including the coastal plain of the Maadam, is thronged with herds of cattle and goats, brought from far distant reaches of Eritrea and the Gash by mountain valleys and mist-cloaked passes to enjoy the winter lushness of the coast. Their masters descend from the hills but rarely, to earn a little tax money by labour in the Delta, or to barter skins and butter for grain, coffee, and their other few necessities in the little dhow-port of Agig, which is the headquarters of their administration. The dwellers in these hills are, for the most part, Tigré-speaking clans belonging to the Beni Amer Nazirate, Almada, Asfada, Wilinnoho, Hamasein, Ad Fadil, Abhasheila, and others even smaller and more fragmentary, who until recently were serfs of the Nabtab aristocracy of the tribe. Living among them also, in the higher and remoter valleys, is a numerous group of To Bedawie-speaking peoples, the Labat, Ad Kokoi, Beit Awat and Libis, whose history is very different and who are of a much purer Hamitic stock.[1]

Before venturing, in the next chapter, to enter upon the debatable ground of Beja origins, it is as well to have clear in

---

[1] The Beni Amer, described more fully in Chapter VIII, are less a tribe than a loosely knit confederation of groups of different origins which, in addition to the small Nabtab caste and its one-time serfs, includes Aflanda, Beit Ma'ala, and Agaiga, who are recent accretions to the Nazirate since 1900. I must disagree here with Crawford's assertion (*The Fung Kingdom of Sennar* (1950), p. 109) that the southern Beni Amer in the main speak Tigré, and those in the north To Bedawie. There is no such geographical dividing line, though it is true that the To Bedawie-speaking clans came originally from farther north and brought the language with them.

the mind that the tribes so described can be classified broadly in three easily distinguishable groups. First, that which contains the Amarar and the Besharin, both of whom might admit to some strain of Kawahla and other Arab blood, and the Hadendowa, who appear since their first emergence as a tribe to have taken wives freely from neighbouring Arab tribes, such as the Kimmeilab, Shukria, Jaaliin and others. In all three, however, Hamitic blood and characteristics unmistakably predominate. It is even more predominant and unmistakable in the To Bedawie-speaking sections of the Beni Amer mentioned above, whom there is reason to believe are possibly the purest in blood of all.

The second group consists entirely of the Tigré-speaking sections of the Beni Amer, who are of original Hamitic stock but diluted since very early times by copious Semitic infusions which have resulted in different language, customs, and racial characteristics.

The third group, the *Gabail Ukhra* (which here includes the Halenga, Hamran, and a few other small tribes), are Beja only in the sense that they are partly so by blood, and almost wholly so in language and custom. They are the descendants of medieval Arab intruders, comparative latecomers to the western shores of the Red Sea, who settled in the Beja country and made good their position by marrying Beja wives. They are for the most part insignificant tribes who, by a wholly un-Beja-like display of industry and business acumen, have prospered both as traders and cultivators. Prior to the advent of the present government they subsisted in such small corners of the Beja country as more powerful tribes did not covet for themselves, and in the Tokar area are centred on the Delta, from which, now that it yields rich revenues from cotton, the ever-expanding Hadendowa with their lust for new pastures and greater living room, would probably long since have expelled them but for the protecting arm of the government.

It may be asked what is the essential difference between those who are classified as true Beja, and those who are not. The latter have, for a period of roughly a thousand years, intermarried continuously with Beja, and in so doing have adopted their language, and most of their customs, while in the former it is admitted that the Hamitic strain has been modified not inconsiderably by Semitic infusions. This being so the two groups should surely show few dissimilarities, and there can be no good reason for discrimination.

The answer is that there is an essential difference, which is unmistakable, and that it is to be found mainly in physical dissimilarity. No one with any local knowledge could doubt for a moment that the Arteiga, for instance, were anything but Arab, and what is more of Himyarite stock. The Kimmeilab might be put down among their Kawahla cousins of Kordofan with little fear of immediate detection as strangers. The Halenga who, it is true, have intermarried much with Arabs, have more Semitic traits than any other, and only of the Shaiab, the nomad cousins of the Arteiga, would it be difficult to say, without special knowledge, that they were not true Beja.

Those tribes, therefore, which can be designated pseudo-Beja are those of known Arab ancestry, in whom almost without exception the physical features and characteristics of the Hamite are lacking.

CHAPTER III

BEJA ORIGINS

The Beja are attributed to Kush, the son of Ham, and emigrated
to the Sudan after the Flood.   AMARAR HISTORY[1]

If it be hardly possible to accept in its entire simplicity the
statement of the Amarar historian above, yet it can be allowed,
and nearly all authorities agree, that the Beja are a Hamitic
people who crossed the Red Sea from Arabia at a very early
date, and settled on the eastern fringes of Africa between the
Nile and the sea; it is the opinion of Johnston that they

were living where they are now when the dynastic Egyptians poured
as a Neolithic conquering host into the Nile valley in Lower Nubia,
and made their way along the narrow ribbon of habitable Egypt
on either side of the Desert Nile.[2]

Rock inscriptions and drawings in the Eastern Desert, so far
as they have been or can be interpreted, show that the earliest
known inhabitants of these regions were a primitive race of
hunters using a large C-shaped bow, well acquainted with such
wild animals as elephants, crocodiles and giraffe, but possessing
very little artistic sense.

They were followed by a Hamitic race of cattle owners (the
early ancestors of the present-day Beja) who inhabited both
the desert and the valley of the Nile. They also were hunters,
using a 3-shaped bow and, possibly, metal-pointed arrows,
who pursued such game as elephant, ibex, wild ass, antelope,
giraffe and ostrich. They were artists of some merit, and some
of their drawings are executed with a high degree of skill.[3]

[1] Translation of an anonymous compilation on the tribal history of the
Amarar to be found in Sudan Government Archives.
[2] *The Colonization of Africa by Alien Races*, pp. 17–18.
[3] Winkler, *Rock Drawings of Southern Upper Egypt*, vol. I (1938). Plate
XX (1) shows a man shooting an ostrich, and also exceedingly well-executed
drawings in outline of ariel, dikdik, oryx, rhinoceros and elephant.

I do not think, therefore, that it can be accepted, as Keane suggests, that the Beja are the true autochthonous element of the Eastern Desert,[1] and it can be fairly concluded, from such evidence as exists, that they are a secondary race of invaders whose first arrival has been dated as early as 4000 B.C., and certainly prior to 2500 B.C., when they appear first to have come to the notice of the Egyptians of the VIth Dynasty.

Seligman reaches the conclusion that the Beja (and more particularly some of the Tigré-speaking sections of the Beni Amer) closely resemble the proto-Egyptians.

It seems that it is justifiable to regard the Beni Amer, the least modified of the Beja tribes, as the modern representatives of the old pre-dynastic Egyptian (and Nubian) stock, and it further appears that the modification undergone by the latter during a period of some 7000 or more years is extremely small.[2]

This conclusion is based on the evidence of comparative physical measurements, supported by local information which, as ever, tends to be inaccurate, and at times is actually misleading.

Seligman's researches have tended to show that in stature and head measurements certain of the Beni Amer and the pre-dynastic Egyptians were remarkably similar, but that other Beja tribes, the Hadendowa, the Amarar, and the Besharin, show signs of foreign admixture which has increased their height and raised their cephalic indices. The table on p. 22 is taken, with minor modifications in arrangement to facilitate comparison, from Murray's article in the *Journal of the Royal Anthropological Society*,[3] which is itself an addendum to Seligman's article referred to above.

From the table it will be seen that the Hadendowa tend to be an inch or so taller than the Beni Amer, and the Besharin slightly taller again; that in length of skulls there is no great divergence (except in the Besharin), but that in breadth the

[1] 'The Ethnology of the Egyptian Sudan', *J.R.A.I.* (1885), p. 101.
[2] 'Some Aspects of the Hamitic Problem in the Anglo-Egyptian Sudan', *J.R.A.S.* No. 43 (1913), pp. 606–7.
[3] 'The Northern Beja', *J.R.A.S.* No. 57 (1927), pp. 40–1.

Beni Amer skull is definitely narrower, and that on the evidence of these measurements the Beni Amer measured are the closest modern approximation among the Beja to the pre-dynastic type of Egyptian. Seligman is further of the opinion that the modification in the original type apparent in other Beja is due to a brachycephalic element which came from the north, and that the Hadendowa particularly show traces both of negro and Armenoid blood.

Tribe	Number	H.L. (mm.)	H.B. (mm.)	Stature (m.)
Early Pre-dynastic Egyptians from Naga el Deir	45	184·8	131·5	1·630 (approx.)
Middle Nubian Group C	123	183·0	134·0	—
Beni Amer	51	183·5	133·75	1·643
Hadendowa	40	182·8	135·8	1·674
Amarar	16	183·6	138·9	1·666
Besharin (Aliab)	30	177·7	135·6	1·680

In selecting the Beni Amer whom he measured Seligman informs us that he chose only 'genuine Beni Amer who all belonged to old and important Tigré-speaking divisions'.[1] It is unfortunate that he does not specify what divisions these were more closely, for the Beni Amer are indeed a very mixed people issuing from many separate racial founts, whom Seligman himself admits to be 'a nation that has arisen from a number of politically distinct elements, rather than a people formed by the cohesion of a number of closely related divisions', and 'whose manners appear to have been softened by the same Semitic cultural influence which has given them a Semitic language'.[2]

If Seligman selected the Tigré-speaking Beni Amer of such sections as the Almada, Wilinnoho, Asfada, or other related clans, he might expect to find a survival of the ancient Hamitic stock modified by Semitic infusions from Saba' and the Hadramaut some 3000–2500 years ago, but since then practically undisturbed. After the decline of the kingdom of Axum in the

[1] Op cit. p. 601.   [2] Op. cit. pp. 600 and 598.

ninth century A.D. these peoples were subdued by conquerors of non-Hamitic origins, but it was an essential part of the caste system which they imposed that there was no intermarriage with their serf peoples. There has therefore been very little physical change (or change of any sort for that matter) in the Beni Amer serf tribes over a period of some thousands of years.

If on the other hand, but as seems improbable, Seligman measured Beni Amer of the clans whom he calls Bedawib (the Ad Kokoi, Beit Awat, Ad el Khasa, etc., most of whom are bilingual in Tigré and To Bedawie) or the Sinkatkinab, Labat,[1] or any other of the To Bedawie-speaking clans whom he mistakenly classes as 'out-liers of the Hadendoa',[2] he would, in my opinion, have discovered the closest modern equivalent of all to the ancient pre-dynastic type, in a people who are widely recognized to be of the oldest and least modified Beja stock of all, in whom almost no foreign elements have been intruded, and who represent a very pure Hamitic type, small, wiry, with level jaws, straight noses, and curly hair, dark olive to black in colour, broad of shoulder and thin of flank, with slim but extraordinarily well-muscled legs. They are a by no means numerous race: there are a considerable number in Eritrea, but in the Sudan they do not number more than about 4000 all told, a shy, primitive, and unapproachable people, living in the remotest hills and glens, and coming but rarely into contact with the world beyond.

As regards the Hadendowa, the negro and Armenoid strain which undoubtedly exists might be explained by the theory of Floyer that the autochthonous inhabitants of the Eastern Desert of Egypt were a race of negroid miners who traded with the

---

[1] The Labat are alleged to have some Hadendowa blood in them, but have a long-standing and bitter feud with the Hadendowa nevertheless. The small Hadoigoboiab section which belongs to this group is almost certainly Hadendowa in origin, and from this and from the fact that the whole group speaks To Bedawie like the Hadendowa, may arise the commonly held misconception of their Hadendowa affinities.

[2] *Op. cit.* p. 600.

Phoenicians, who had affinities with the present-day Nuba of Kordofan, and who were expelled by the dynastic Egyptians. The Beja and this now extinct negroid race shared the country between them and, as they seemed to be on amicable terms with one another, no doubt intermarried, 'un race de mineurs négroids exploitait les mines d'or, et les Blemmyes leur apportaient la nourriture, et pourvoyaient autres nécessités de leur vie'.[1] It is an attractive theory, but it does not seem to be based on any conclusive evidence, and the origins of the negroid element in the Hadendowa must remain a matter for conjecture. My own view is that it introduced itself later rather than earlier, otherwise other northern Beja tribes, such as the Besharin and Amarar, would display similar traits, which they do not.

As for the brachycephalic element in the northern Beja, Seligman, after discussing the possibility that it came from across the Red Sea, dismisses it in favour of a northern origin. In doing so he ignores the fact that since the seventh century A.D. if no earlier, there has been an almost constant infiltration into the Beja country north of Khor Baraka of Semitic peoples who have intermarried extensively with the Beja, and who thus cannot have been without influence on their physical development, and thus give reason for the taller stature and broader heads of the northern Beja tribes.

There are repeated references in Arab tribal legends in the Sudan to an invasion from the Yemen which took place in the seventh century, or even rather earlier, and which cannot but refer to the pre-Islamic influx of the people later to be known as the Bellou, or Hadareb, into the Atbai, Gwineb, and Maadam. This was followed in the ninth and tenth centuries by settlement of gold-hunting Arabs, mainly of the Rabi'a, who also intermarried extensively with the Beja, and by some Kawahla elements in the thirteenth century. During all this time also such small tribes as the Halenga, Arteiga, Ashraf and Hassanab had been settling in different parts of the Beja country (entering usually by Suakin) and intermarrying so extensively with the

[1] *Études sur le Nord Etbai* (1893), p. 77.

PLATE II

A HADENDOWI CAMELMAN

local inhabitants that they came to adopt their language and customs, all of which is in contradiction to Seligman's conclusion that 'where the Semitic and Hamitic have mixed the latter have ever adopted the language of the former, and where mixed people have arisen I think it can be said that they are more Arab than Hamitic.'[1]

Moreover, ever since the emergence of the Hadendowa, Amarar and Besharin as tribal entities (of mixed but preponderantly Hamitic stock) in the fifteenth and sixteenth centuries they, and especially the Hadendowa, have continued to marry wives of non-Beja origin. The Atbai Besharin had taken wives from the Ababda, as the Atbara Besharin have done from the Jaaliin and Merefab, and have given them their daughters in marriage, and various Hadendowa sections such as the Bushariab, Gemilab, and Ger'ib, to name but three, trace descent from a Shukri, a Jaali and a Fungawi respectively.

It is not surprising, therefore, that Seligman's researches in the early years of this century should have discovered considerable modifications in the original type, and I think the Beja of today can best be described as a Hamito-Semitic people who are divided into two main groups—a southern one of purer Hamitic strain, but speaking a Semitic language, which has only very recently emerged from an agelong serfdom, and a northern one, less pure in blood, but speaking a Hamitic language, and displaying typical Hamitic characteristics much more clearly than the southern group. The warrior individualism of the north finds no counterpart in the south, where the Beni Amer clans, unless well organized and led, are apt to be sheeplike and meek. It is unlikely that archaeological research in the Beja country will yield much of interest to the historian or anthropologist, or throw any brilliantly revealing light on the question of Beja origins. There are few remains, and fewer still of any great antiquity. The towers to the north of Port Sudan, and the castles of Derheib can be attributed with some certainty to the medieval Arab exploiters of the gold

[1] *Op. cit.* p. 603.

mines. The tower tombs of the great necropolis of Maman and other kindred sites are almost certainly medieval also, but of uncertain origin.[1] The remains at Isaderheib, behind Agig, are of greater interest, and may very probably be Ptolemaic, and finally there are a few scattered rock pictures and inscriptions, and the unique fish-tail tombs of Erkowit whose age and origin have yet to be determined.

[1] See also Paul, 'Ancient Tombs in Kassala Province', *S.N.R.* vol. XXXIII (1) (1952).

CHAPTER IV

THE GOLD AND INCENSE LANDS
(2500–50 B.C.)

And I have brought thee splendid gold,
The strong man's joy, refined and cold.   FLECKER

When gold was first discovered in the hills inhabited by the
ancient Beja is not exactly known, but it has been placed by
some authorities as early as 3000–2500 B.C., and it is possible
that the first expeditions to the eastern deserts for exploitation
of gold were sent out under the powerful Vth Dynasty (2745–
2625 B.C.).[1] About this time also, in the reign of Pepi II,
c. 2644 B.C., an expedition under a captain called Sebni was sent
farther south and east to what was then known as the God's Land
of Punt which, besides ivory, gold and skins, brought back a
rich store of the resins and incense so essential to the rites and
mysteries of ancient Egypt. From then on, for nearly seven hundred years, there was a steady and profitable trade in aromatics,
frankincense and myrrh, across Tigré to the river ports of the
Nile valley. The famous expedition of Queen Hatepshut, of the
brilliant and able XVIIIth Dynasty, which rediscovered Punt
about 1450 B.C. brought back with it an astonishing cargo
containing

all goodly fragrant woods of God's Land, heaps of myrrh-resin,
fresh myrrh trees, ebony, pure ivory, green gold of Amu, cinnamon
wood...ihmut incense, sonter incense, eye cosmetic, apes, monkeys,
dogs, skins of the southern panther....[2]

About the same time also the Pharaohs became interested in
the development of the trade in precious stones from the Red
Sea islands, and St John's Island, whence were exported peridots

[1] According to Floyer the earliest workers for gold were a race of negroid
stock, distinct from the pastoral Hamitic Beja, who were prior to, or con-
temporaneous with, the dynastic Egyptians who eventually drove them from
the mines by armed aggression.
[2] Breasted, *Ancient Records of Egypt*, vol. II, p. 109.

and chrysolites rather than the real topaz, has been identified as the 'Topaz Isle' of the ancients. Tortoise-shell was also in great demand, and as a luxury trade was to have a long life, extending well into the Middle Ages.

Under the early Middle Empire (the XIIth–XIVth Dynasties, 2000–1580 B.C.) such mines as were then known, those of Nubia, and in the Eastern Desert to the north, approximately, of the present Sudan-Egyptian frontier, were worked to capacity, and to this period belongs the first known portrait of a Bejawi, represented unmistakably on a XIIth Dynasty tomb chapel at Meir in Upper Egypt, 'showing the slender limbs, pointed nose, retracted abdomen, broad chest, and the great shock of hair of the modern Beshari or Hadendowi'.[1]

Under the Bedawin XVth and XVIth Dynasties the mines do not appear to have been worked, but their exploitation was continued with renewed energy under the New Empire. Thutmose I, a Pharaoh of the XVIIIth Dynasty, considered the gold trade of sufficient importance to justify appointment of a 'Governor of the Gold Country of Coptos', and it is alleged that Thutmose III about 1420 B.C. drew revenue of 2400 pounds weight of gold from the mines of Nubia and the Eastern Desert. So much gold was there indeed in Egypt, from the Nubian, Sinaitic and Eastern Desert mines, that it was for long regarded as an inferior metal to silver, and was much more commonly in use up to about 1800 B.C.

By about 1300 B.C., however, the supply was falling off, and sank to as low as 600–800 pounds weight annually. Seti I of the XIXth Dynasty (1320–1300 B.C.) therefore took steps to restore the supply: his expeditions pushed farther south in search of new lodes, and attempted unsuccessfully to develop the Derheib mine in the Wadi Allagi (Akaita), and it may be to him that we owe production of the earliest known map in the world, the Turin Papyrus, which is almost certainly a representation of the Derheib mine. He improved the route between

[1] D. Newbold, 'The Beja Tribes of the Red Sea Hills', in *The Anglo-Egyptian Sudan from Within* (ed. Hamilton, 1935), p. 145.

the mines and the Nile valley by opening new wells, but the well which he dug in the Wadi Allagi ran dry with disastrous results for the mining community, and the successful exploitation of the mine was left to his successor Rameses II (1307–1233 B.C.) who dug a new well and improved the old one; and also to Amenemhat III, who built a fort at Dakka, where the Wadi Allagi joins the Nile, for the protection of the gold caravans, and as an entrepôt for shipment of gold to Memphis.

The Red Sea hills, as far south approximately as the present Port Sudan-Atbara railway line, are full of ancient workings, of which no less than about eighty-five important ones have been charted within recent years. The workings consist of shafts of as much as 150 ft. or more, in which wooden props were used to support any weaknesses in the adit. The ore was crushed in hand-mills, examples of which are still to be found, together with traces of primitive but none the less effective washing tables, though some of these no doubt belong to the medieval Arab period. The conditions under which gold was extracted were appalling almost beyond description. The Pharaohs sent to the mines their political enemies, criminals, captives of war, and all who had in any way incurred their displeasure. This human material, whose only release from misery and toil beneath the whip of brutal overseers was by death, was expended prodigally and callously, and with regard to nothing provided that the output of gold was maintained. Large garrisons were maintained at the most important mines, and the expedition which Rameses III sent to the Eastern Desert to search for gold about 1180 B.C. consisted of upwards of 8000 persons, including 5000 soldiers, 2000 crown slaves, and 800 foreign captives. Camels being then unknown, donkeys were used for transport of stores and gold to and from the mines, and caravans were escorted through the desert by Nubian soldiery called *matchai*.

The Pharaohs of the XXth Dynasty, and especially Rameses III (1198–1167 B.C.), continued the exploitation not only of the gold-mines but also of the incense trade, which became of more importance than ever, for all Egypt desired to be 'perfumed with myrrh and frankincense, with all powders of the merchant'.[1] But her power was in decline, and after the fall of the XXth Dynasty expeditions to Punt were no longer sent out, and the trade routes to the Nile and the canals connecting it with the Red Sea fell into decay and disuse.

As noted above, the Pharaohs found it necessary to garrison the mines with large numbers of troops (usually foreign mercenaries) partly to control the mining communities of slaves and captives and to safeguard the gold, and partly to defend them against the attacks of marauding Beja, though according to Strabo they were at that time neither warlike nor numerous. The records of ancient Egypt make very little mention of the peoples of the Eastern Desert. The Buka, a people not directly identifiable, are mentioned in some inscriptions, and it is possible also that the Anu, the bowmen of the deserts which surround Egypt, were in part a Beja people.

The Pharaohs made no attempt at proper pacification and administration of the desert tribes, and were content to garrison the mines, and to keep the local population in check by occasional plundering expeditions which carried off their cattle and harried them to a proper state of subjection. Except for its gold the country was barren and useless, though probably rather less so than now, and the Beja, a thinly scattered, poorly armed, nomadic, and still very primitive pastoral people, cannot have been very formidable in war. The Pharaohs had many more powerful enemies with whom to contend, there was nothing about the Beja which seemed to them to merit any particular attention, and it is not until about 200 B.C. that they were given more than the most cursory mention.

It has been suggested that in the Erembes of Homer we have first historical mention of the people of the Eastern Desert later to be known as Blemmyes and Beja:

I came to Cyprus in Phoenicia, and to the Egyptians:
And among the Ethiopians, and the Sidonians, and the Erembes.[2]

[1] Song of Solomon, iii, 6.   [2] *Odyssey*, Book IV.

The passage relates to Menalaeus' visit to Egypt, to his sojourn on the borderlands of Ethiopia (where were possibly Sidonian colonies trading with the farther south), and to his acquisition of great wealth in gold and ivory. It is by no means impossible that the Erembes are the same as the Sembritae, a generic name used to describe the nomad peoples beyond the confines of Egypt, among whom were the ancient Beja. Any closer connection must be regarded as being beyond the bounds of sober acceptance.

Heliodorus, bishop of Emesa, who wrote a history and description of Ethiopia in the fourth century A.D., states that the Beja (Blemmyes) were subject to Meroë and that they fought as allies of the XXVth Dynasty kings against Persia and were released from payment of tribute for fourteen years in return for their services. Nastasenen of Meroë is said to have raided the Eastern Desert gold-mines five times about 290 B.C. and to have been rewarded with 800 troy pounds of gold, gold dust, and 1,250,000 head of cattle. Even allowing that rainfall was heavier and pastures greener and more permanent in those days, it is unlikely that the country ever supported even a quarter of that number, unless of course sheep and goats are included. The present-day cattle population is probably rather less than 175,000 head.

As Egypt fell sick the mines were abandoned; for nearly eight hundred years the Eastern Desert and the hills between the Nile and the sea lapsed into age-long obscurity, and it is not until about 300 B.C., when the captains of the Lagid Dynasty began to explore the coast southwards, that any more is heard of them.

When Alexander of Macedon died in 323 B.C. the empire which he had created was divided among his generals, Egypt falling to the share of Ptolemy, called Soter, to distinguish him from his descendants, all of whom bore the same name. Under him and his immediate successors the wealth and power of Egypt revived, and expeditions for trade and exploration were sent down the Red Sea which re-opened the trade routes, and established markets and watering stations along the coast. Berenice was founded in 275 B.C. under Ptolemy II, Philadelphus, Ptolemais Theron (Agig) in 285 B.C. and Berenice the Golden (Adulis) rather later in the reign of Ptolemy III, Euergetes.[1]

Both the Berenices developed into prosperous ports dealing in ivory, gums, tortoise-shell, ebony, spices and pearls, and Adulis also acquired fame as a slave market. Ptolemais Theron was never a great general market, and it was moreover, as its name ('of the hunts') implies, founded for a particular purpose, since it lay on the edge of the great Nubian forest where elephants abounded. Alexander's generals had been greatly impressed by the effectiveness of the war elephants which they had encountered in India, and the Ptolemies sought industriously but unsuccessfully to train the African elephant for similar purposes. Elephants were at that time numerous in the immediate hinterland, in the valleys of the Baraka, Langeib and Gash, and Ptolemais was founded as a hunting base and port for shipment of captured elephants to Egypt.[2]

It is recorded that Ptolemy II, Philadelphus, sent a captain called Eumedes to fortify the station, and posted there a garrison of Pisidian slingers to counter the attacks of the local Beja bowmen, together with officials and artisans who built temples and houses and laid out the adjacent lands for cultivation. Ptolemy II also endeavoured in vain to persuade the local inhabitants to abstain from eating elephant flesh. The ridge of Isaderheib, a mile or so inland from the little modern port of Agig, which has yet to be examined authoritatively by experts, is rich in what may prove to be the remains of this Ptolemaic settlement to supplement the few references to the elephant trade in the inscriptions and documents which have survived.

Much ingenuity and labour was employed in the capture of

[1] As a result of the difficulty of beating up the Red Sea against the north wind, and of the treacherous nature of its coast, ports were sought as far south as possible whence goods might be transported without too much danger or difficulty to the Nile.

[2] Elephants were still to be found in Khor Baraka within fifty miles of the sea within living memory, i.e. up to about 1890–1900.

THE GOLD AND INCENSE LANDS

elephants and their transport by sea in galleys specially built for the purpose. These were then shipped to Berenice of the Troglodytes, and thence marched across the desert to the Nile at Coptos or Ombi, the transports which shipped them north returning with corn for the garrisons of the hunting stations dotted along the Troglodyte and Somali coasts. In the Wadi Abad, on the route between Berenice and the Nile, there is a rough rock drawing of an elephant beside an inscription in which an anonymous Dorian offers prayers for his safe return from an elephant hunt in the farther south.[1] An inscription of Ptolemy III, Euergetes, deciphered from the Monumentum Adulitanum, records that, 'he set out into Asia with infantry, cavalry, and elephants from Ethiopia and the land of the Troglodytes, which he and his father had first captured there, and brought to Egypt and trained in war' and finally there is the fragmentary dedication to Ares, God of the Hunts, by Alexander, General of the Elephant Hunt in the reign of Ptolemy IV, Philopater, which reads:

On behalf of King Ptolemy and Queen Arsinoë, and Ptolemy, son of the divine Philopater, descended from Ptolemy and Berenice, daughter of the divine Euergetes, to Ares, Bringer of Victory, Fortunate in the Chase, Alexander, son of Sindaeos the Orannean, who was commissioned in succession to Charymortos, the General who instituted the Hunt of the Elephants, and Apoasis, son of Miorbollus the Eteanian, Captain, with all the soldiers serving under him. . . .[2]

African elephants, however, were difficult to train, and temperamental in action, so that their export was discontinued either in the reign of Ptolemy IV or of his successor Ptolemy V, Epiphanes. Convincing and final proof of their unsuitability may have come at the battle of Raphia in 217 B.C. in which, although Ptolemy Philopater was victorious, his elephants, of which he is said to have had seventy-three, were no match

---

[1] Weigall, *Travels in the Upper Egyptian Desert* (1909), p. 163.
[2] Translated from the original given in Mahaffy, *The Ptolemaic Dynasty* (1898), p. 183.

for the Asian ones of Antiochus III, and ran away without engaging.

The early Lagids, apart from reviving the Red Sea trade and experimenting in the use of war elephants, also re-opened the mines in the Eastern Desert, which were worked again for gold up to the first century B.C., whence the output is alleged at one time to have exceeded that of XXth Dynasty times. The methods by which they were exploited were no different and no less brutal than those employed by the Pharaohs:

The Kings of Egypt [wrote Diodorus Siculus] condemn vast multitudes to the mines who are notorious criminals, prisoners of war, and persons convicted by false accusation....Not only the individuals themselves, but even whole families are doomed to this labour, with a view to punishing the guilty and profiting by their toil....All are driven to their work by the lash, until at last, overcome by the intolerable weight of their afflictions, they die in the midst of their toil.[1]

The later Lagids were in the main an effeminate and depraved set of weaklings, who allowed the ports and the roads through the desert to fall into disrepair. The water supplies of the mines were neglected, and they were finally abandoned about 40 B.C.

Although the Ptolemies had but aped the Pharaohs in their exploitation of the mines, and their settlements on the coast were but trading stations and forts for the protection and use of the Indian and Arabian trade, and little contact appears to have been made with the indigenous inhabitants, yet rather more is now known about them. Contemporary accounts relied largely on travellers' tales, and must be accepted with reserve, more especially when so well-informed and so balanced a chronicler as Diodorus Siculus, in the course of his description of the people of these coasts, can record that the sun at midday is there so hot that two men standing side by side cannot see each other because of the density of the air, and that meat in a pot is cooked at once by the heat of the sun. To Pliny they

[1] Diodorus, Book III. He quotes largely from Agatharchides of Cnidus, tutor of Ptolemy X (c. 170–120 B.C.).

34

were a headless people with eyes and ears sunk below the level
of their shoulders and even to less credulous writers they with
the Nuba were merely the Ethiopians who lived beyond Syene.[1]

It may be accepted, therefore, that the writers of the time were
for the most part as largely devoid of accuracy as they were
guilty of picturesque exaggeration, yet there is general agreement that the inhabitants of the eastern deserts were, in the
main, a cave-dwelling people, armed with bows and arrows, and
living under the most grossly primitive conditions. They are
referred to frequently as Troglodytes, a name given to them by
Agatharchides on account of their cave-dwelling habits, and in
this he was copied by nearly all classical writers. Floyer dis-
agrees, and asserts that 'Les Troglodytes seraient des mineurs
d'or et constructeurs de caves, non des habitants de caves'.[2]
To which tribes or groups the name properly applied was a
matter of some doubt. Herodotus, writing as early as 450 B.C.,
mentions the Ichthyophagi or Fish-Eaters, who lived between
Elephantine (Assuan) and the Red Sea, and who may also have
been cave-dwellers. Later writers distinguish between Troglodytes and Ichthyophagi and say that the latter were the
most primitive of all the desert tribes. Diodorus Siculus
(c. 140 B.C.) says of them: 'They go naked...and have their
wives in common,...and like other fish-eating people they do
not drink. They live in caves, tents of grass, under trees, or in
holes dug in the sea moss.'[3] He mentions also their habit of
burying their dead on hill-tops by casting stones over them,
a not over-exaggerated description of a Beja burial of today,
and says that they live on milk boiled with blood. Their weapons
were round shields, clubs, and bows and arrows. Agatharchides
remarks on their custom of never allowing a living creature,
human or animal, to die a natural death, and all, men and cattle

---

[1] 'Accusations of credulity and inaccuracy were freely made and the second
and third hand compilers on whom we depend have left but a confused record
of the country.' (Crowfoot, 'The Island of Meroë', *Arch. Survey of Egypt*
(1911), p. 31.)

[2] *Études sur le Nord Etbai* (1893), p. vi.   [3] Diodorus, III, 15.

alike, were put to death when senility or fatal illness overtook them. Also mentioned are the Agriophagi or Acridophagi (Flesh-Eaters or Locust-Eaters) and the Mosophagi, or those who browse like cattle.[1]

It must be concluded, therefore, that the Beja of Dynastic and Ptolemaic times, and until even later, whether they be described as eaters of flesh, fish, locusts, or even of grass, were in the main a primitive pastoral people, dwellers in caves where such existed, and in shelters of grass or skins where they did not, and that Diodorus' description of them can be accepted as the best of contemporary accounts. There still exists a belief among some Beja tribes of today that their remote ancestors were Troglodytes inhabiting underground dwellings, of which the many circular mounds (most probably tombs) to be found throughout their country were the overground entrances, and that the description of them as a shepherd people who lived in caves is an accurate one.[2] Those most closely situated to the Nile valley cannot, however, have been entirely without sophistication, as there exists a delightful late Ptolemaic document which records the punishment of two inhabitants of Elephantine (Assuan) for, among other delinquencies, 'drinking with the Blemmyes'.[3]

Nevertheless, the three hundred years of Ptolemaic exploitation of the gold mines and of the Red Sea trade were productive, in so far as the Beja were concerned, of far greater and more obvious results than the much longer period of similar exploitation by Dynastic Egypt. The Greek mercenaries whom the Ptolemies employed to garrison and administer the mines and ports, and the merchants who traded in them, were an adventurous type, and the legend of them is still green along the coast as the Rum, a white race of giant stature, who intermarried with the local tribes and developed the country with

---

[1] *Periplus of the Erythrean Sea*, translated by Schoff (1912), p. 22.

[2] Linant de Bellefonds appears to have excavated one of these mounds and records the finding of human remains a little below the true surface of the ground (*L'Etbaye* (1884), p. 48).

[3] Griffith, 'Dodgson Papers', *P.S.B.A.* vol. XXXI, p. 100.

energy and ability, digging cisterns (traces of some of which can still be found), encouraging agriculture, and adapting themselves generally to the life of the country. To them, and to their penetration into the hills of Tigré, by force of arms under a Ptolemaic captain as local legend insists, or by more peaceable means, may be due the rise of the mysterious kingdom of Axum.

Further evidence of their influence was the adoption by many Beja tribes of the state religion of Isis and Serapis.[1] Religion has at all times sat but lightly on the Beja conscience, and their observance of creed and ritual has never been very exact. Throughout their long history they have shown remarkable aptitude for adoption of strange religions, and in their time have been successively idolators, ancestor- and demon-worshippers, devotees of Isis, Serapis and Priapus, worshippers of Sabaean gods of sky and earth, Jacobite Christians, and lastly Mohammedans. Such is still their faith, but Burckhardt remarks that the Hadendowa and Besharin, though nominally Moslems, 'perform none of the rites prescribed by that religion'. Such adaptability in a people otherwise so impervious to change is surprising, but I can only record it as a fact. They are certainly no fanatics, and though they have been faithful to Islam for some four centuries now, were they to find it expedient for any reason to change their religion I am convinced they would do so with few scruples, and become outward observing Confucians with a very good grace.

[1] According to Procopius (*De Bello Persico*, I, xix) the Blemmyes worshipped Isis, Osiris and Priapus, and all the gods of Greeks, but he adds that they also offered human sacrifices to the Sun, possibly in his manifestation as Mandulis, one of their particular deities.

CHAPTER V

THE SABAEANS
AND THE KINGDOM OF AXUM
(700 B.C.–A.D. 750)

The land shadowing with wings, which is beyond
the rivers of Ethiopia.   ISAIAH, xviii, 1

At some date many years before Christ, which has been placed
by some authorities as early as 1000 B.C., and by others as late
as 600 B.C., the Sabaeans, who were then the dominant power
in Southern Arabia, and who inhabited the high mountain
valleys of the Hadramaut, crossed the Red Sea in search of
trade, and occupying first the coastal islands such as Dahlak,
settled finally in what are now the Tigrean highlands lying
partly in Ethiopia and partly in Eritrea.

The Sabaeans were a younger branch of the great tribe of
Joktan which had conquered much of Southern Arabia about
1800 B.C. but which in the course of time had been largely
absorbed by the more ancient Cushite race which they had
subjected. Nevertheless those who could boast Joktan descent
were regarded as a sacred ruling caste, living on the labour of
a Cushite peasantry, who were herdsmen, tillers of the soil,
and gatherers of incense.

When in the course of their expansion the Sabaeans crossed
the sea, and from their trading settlements gradually penetrated
into the mountainous regions of the interior, they found conditions very similar to those which they had left behind them in
Arabia—a high, well-watered country with a pleasant climate,
only thinly populated by a number of primitive pastoral tribes
of ancient Beja stock. The first settlers were traders, dealing in
ivory, gold, aromatics, tortoise-shell and ebony, but as their
wealth and power increased it cannot be doubted that they
acquired an overlordship over the indigenous tribes who became
to them as the Cushite peoples of the Hadramaut had been to

38

their forebears, 'hewers of wood and drawers of water'. On them they imposed not only their language and their religious beliefs, but also the feudal conception of society imported from their homeland, some measure of their artistic ability, and a not inconsiderable admixture of their blood as the result of inter-marriage and concubinage.

Thus at a very early date the southern Beja were impressed with the characteristics which today distinguish them from those of the north, and by the time that the Blemmyes and other Beja tribes in the eastern deserts had begun to make themselves felt on the confines of Roman Egypt about A.D. 250 the hill Beja in the south had already become a people different in language and blood, long fettered and docile under alien rule.

How long the domination of the original Sabaean settlers lasted is not known. The ruins of at least one of their cities was discovered by Bent at Yeha, and has been identified as Ava, which flourished in the eighth or seventh century B.C., and there are probably others, as yet undiscovered, hidden in the hills and valleys of Tigré and Hamasien. They appear not to have ex-tended their influence very widely, and to have been an oligarchy of traders and pastoralists, content with the profits of their ventures, the increase of their flocks, and the labour of their serfs.

In the century which elapsed between 350 and 250 B.C., how-ever, the first Ptolemies of the Lagid Dynasty in Egypt sent their navies down the Red Sea, founding trading stations by the way, one of which was Berenice the Golden, or Adulis, founded in 275 B.C. by Ptolemy Philadelphus. The writer of the *Periplus of the Erythrean Sea* records that about A.D. 50–60 Adulis exported ivory, tortoise-shell, and rhinoceros horn, in return for a very much longer list of imports which included cloth of various sorts and colours, brass for coinage and orna-mentation, wine, oil, copper, glass, and a special selection of luxury goods for the king of Axum. More than trade goods, however, travelled along the route which led to Axum and beyond, and Greek and Egyptian influences were strongly at work in the years which immediately preceded the rise of that kingdom in the heart of the Tigrean hills. It is not, however, until about the time of the Roman occupation of Egypt, or rather later, that there is evidence of the strange and barbaric power, which at some time between 50 B.C. and A.D. 50 emerged in the highlands of Tigré and survived for some 800 years, yet of which almost nothing is known, and which still possesses all the fascination of a problem yet unsolved.

Its origins, like everything else about it, are always likely to be a matter for conjecture and doubt. By some it is believed that a local dynasty, emerging from a feudal society of petty chiefs, nobles and serfs, suddenly made itself supreme, and that this again was made possible by control of the principal trade routes from Adulis whereby wealth, weapons, and some measure of outside assistance all contributed to the final result. By others it is believed that the original Sabaean overlords were displaced by fresh invaders from Southern Arabia, the Habasat, from whose name is derived that of Abyssinia. It is said that in 75 B.C. the Habasat in Arabia made an alliance with Saba' against the growing power of the rival kingdoms of Himyar and Hadramaut. In the struggle which followed the weaker alliance was defeated, and the Habasat were expelled from their homes:

despoiled of their incense terraces in Arabia, and of their commercial activities at Guardafui, the Habasat sought a new home; and in the Tigré highlands built their stronghold...which soon became the city of Axum.[1]

That there was such an influx at this time is extremely probable, but it is much less possible to say whether or not the newcomers were the founders of Axum.[2] It is possible that they took a leading part in the creation of the kingdom and the direction of its policy, all of which might go to explain its long-continued hostility towards the Himyarite kingdom in the

[1] Schoff, *op. cit.* p. 63.
[2] Kammerer (*Essaie sur l'Histoire antique d'Abyssinie* (1926), p. 43) is of the opinion that the Habasat migration took place several centuries earlier, and that as early as 100 B.C. they had invaded Southern Arabia from Africa.

Yemen which was to end only with the final destruction of the latter. Local tradition, which is diffuse and not to be relied on, nevertheless holds strongly to a story of conquest by a fair race of unusual stature, the Rum, and the foundation of the kingdom by their descendants after intermarriage with the daughters of local chiefs. In this there is possibly a distorted echo of an expedition by one of the captains of Ptolemy Euergetes (247–232 B.C.) which is believed to have reduced much of Tigré to subjection, and though the conquest was not lasting, it is possible that its effect on local conditions was considerable, and that Greek adventurers had something to do with the rise of the new kingdom.

All three theories are tenable, but about the date of the Habasat incursion into Africa there is considerable dispute. Some authorities, such as Budge, believe them to have been among the earliest Semitic invaders, bringing superior culture into a land inhabited previously only by primitive pastorals; others believe that they are comparatively late comers, arriving only a century or so before Christ, and re-invigorating or displacing the early Sabaean stock.

Whatever the truth, the kingdom was well established by about A.D. 60, when first mention of it is made by the anonymous writer of the *Periplus*, and in the words of Budge its rise 'synchronises with the downfall of the kingdom of Napata through the defeat of Queen Candace by Petronius, the Roman prefect of Egypt, about 23 B.C. and the conquest of the Sabaeans by the Himyarites about the same time'.[1] The first known king, believed by Dillman to be the successor of the founder of the kingdom, was the miserly but cultured Zoscales, who was acquainted with Greek, and under him and his successors the kingdom was to grow and flourish until it extended its authority over all the country between Khor Baraka and the Straits of Bab el Mandeb, and at the height of its power reached south to Azanea on the Indian Ocean, and west to the Nile valley, carried its arms among the northern Beja as far as the confines of

[1] Budge, *A History of Ethiopia* (1928), vol. I, p. 236.

Egypt, and finally overthrew the rival kingdom of Himyar in the Yemen.

There are no authentic chronicles of the kingdom. Little reliance can be placed in the lists of kings derived from Ethiopian MSS., and reproduced by Bruce, Salt, Budge, and others. They are designed principally to prove the antiquity and venerable descent of the Solomonid line of Ethiopia, and the period which has reference to Axum, from the Nativity onwards, has rightly been described by Budge as 'semi-historical; Abyssinian history only begins. . . in 1268 or 1270'.[1] It is my belief that the origins of the so-called line of Solomon are to be found in Shoa, and the last ruler to hold sway over Axum before its final destruction by the Zagwé in the ninth century was in fact a Shoan. Axum was not, therefore, as the Ethiopian chronicles maintain, the forerunner of the present Ethiopian state, and the inclusion of its rulers in the Solomonid line of Ethiopia has no justification in fact.

Such little knowledge as we possess comes from legends and fragmentary inscriptions, yet even from these some sort of picture may be drawn. The kings of Axum ruled over a feudal state in which a small, cultured, noble caste lived on the labour of its serfs, the vastly more numerous but primitive Beja whose original Hamitic blood was by now much diluted by Semitic infusions, a submissive pastoral people, interested only in the herding of their flocks and the harvesting of their occasional crops, a people in blood, habit, and occupation not greatly different from the inhabitants of the same area today. The life-blood of the kingdom, however, was the trade which flowed through its ports, and which was the main interest of the nobility; from which also came the wealth and power which enabled its barbarically splendid and semi-cultured rulers to rear vast monuments to their gods, and to carry their arms victoriously to the Nile valley and to the opposite shores of the Red Sea.

The great monoliths of Axum, described in some detail by

[1] *Op. cit.* p. 220.

42

Bent and other travellers, remain an architectural puzzle which is unlikely to be resolved until their site is more closely examined and much hitherto undiscovered material revealed. That they could have been carved only by highly skilled workmen, and erected only by equally highly skilled technicians with the help of almost limitless manpower seems certain. It seems certain also that they were erected in adoration of whatever gods the Axumites then worshipped, the Sun, Aster, Medir, Mahrem, and 'all the host of heaven', and that they were used as places of sacrifice. But whether the workmen who made and erected them were of native breed, or came from beyond the seas, or from Egypt, is yet unknown. Architecturally they show traces of. Indian inspiration, and have superficial resemblances to Indian temples known to have been erected at very much the same time, i.e. some time after the Nativity, but prior to 340. But in execution they are less Indian than Egyptian, and it is fascinating to suppose that here in the mountains of Tigré designers and artisans from India and Egypt may have met and co-operated in the erection of these vast monuments to the glory of the strange gods of savage kings. Kammerer considers that they are funerary monuments, erected in the pre-Christian era, possibly in the early part of the reign of Aizanas, and that though in conception they may owe something to Egypt, in execution and design they are Arabian—'si l'idée égyptienne de l'obélisque a pu inspirer leur edification... si même la technique d'un pareil travail a du être copiée sur celle des Pharoans, par contre l'ornamentation ne doit rien à l'Égypte et paraît tout entière Arabique'.[1]

Only a few of the kings are known to us with any certainty: Zoscales of the miserly habits and Greek scholarship; Aphilas, possibly the unknown king whose inscription was deciphered from the Monumentum Adulitanum; Aizanas, who destroyed the Kushites and the remnants of Meroë in 356, and who became a Christian; Asbaha, who sent expeditions against the Yemen, and who reigned from 514 to 542; and Armah, who gave sanc-

[1] Kammerer, *op. cit.* p. 130.

43

tuary to the persecuted companions of Mohammed. Nearly all of them are known from their inscriptions, grandiloquent effusions written often in Sabaean and Greek as well as Ethiopic characters; some from their coinage, of which specimens are still to be found; and a few others from historical references of the time. The inscriptions are few, fragmentary, and incomplete, beginning nearly always with a recitation of the name and titles of the king who inspired them: 'A...King of Axum, of Himyar, Reidan, Habasat, and Saba', of Silh and Tiyam, and of the Kasu and the Beja, King of Kings, Son of Mahrem (Ares) the Unconquerable....'

These titles are so generally applied that they can be accepted as little more than a traditional and laudistic formula, and are by no means evidence that the kings were *de facto* rulers of all the lands and peoples mentioned any more than the kings of England, who quartered the lilies on their shields, were kings of France. There is no doubt that Axum at the height of its power did extend its boundaries to include kingdoms and peoples far afield, and the Adulis inscription, commemorating the conquests of an unknown king (possibly Aphilas) mentions Adawa, Semien, and Agamé in the adjacent highlands, the coastal regions of the present Danakil country, and tribes such as the Beja and Atalmo: 'I crossed the Takazze (Atbara) and overthrew Ava...I overthrew the Atalmo and the Beja and all the people who camp round them, and I marched to Egypt.' He mentions also such tribes as the Atagau, Sogaiet, and Agaazeinat. The latter are identifiable possibly as the Geez, from whom the language of the Ethiopic scriptures takes its name, the Sogaiet survive as a small clan of the Beni Amer, and the Atagau (Tigré: Ad Agau) can be none other than the Beja tribe of that name which had inhabited the western hills of Tigré from very early times, and there is a section of the Beit Ma'ala, the Ad Alma (the People of the Crocodile) whose name approximates to the Atalmo.

The dates of Aphilas (if it was he) are unknown, possibly late third or early second century B.C. but the inscription is of interest for two reasons. First for its record of the destruction of the old Sabaean settlement of Ava,[1] and secondly for the first time there is mention of the Hamitic tribes of the Red Sea coast by the name by which they are still generally known, the Beja, though it is clear that here it applies only to the tribes of the north-eastern deserts, the area today inhabited by the Amarar, Besharin and Hadendowa, and not to all of those whom we now call Beja.[2] In these campaigns the king must have used large numbers of his serf subjects as foot-soldiers and camp-followers, so that his raids against the northern Beja can be regarded as the first known incidents in the long history of that warfare, raid and counter-raid, which still continues along the line of the Atbara, the Baraka, and the Gash.[3]

An inscription of Ela Amida, the father of the more famous Aizanas, records that he had trouble with the Kasu over payment of tribute, for he says: 'they hid their camels from me'. The Kasu have been identified with the people of Meroë, and may have included also some of the now extinct Beja tribes, the Haffara, etc., who lived in the triangle of desert country between the river Atbara and the westward loop of the Nile at Abu Hamed. Meroë by this time had fallen into decay, and her hold over her subject peoples must have been lost.

Aizanas, who followed Ela Amida on the throne in about 330, was the greatest of the kings who ruled in Axum, a warrior and authoritarian who suffered no disobedience to his word: 'He who said I will obey was safe: he who refused was put to death.' From the point of view of Beja history his inscriptions are of exceptional interest, as one of them records a revolt of the Beja

[1] McCrindle, editing the *Christian Topography of Cosmas*, considers that it was Adowa (Ad Ava) which was destroyed, and not Ava (p. 61, n. 1). Of the two I incline to Ava as being a known ancient settlement of which traces still exist, whereas there are none at Adowa.

[2] A Coptic fragment ascribed to Epiphanius (315–403) mentions Axumites, Adulites and Bougaioi=Beja.

[3] He also crossed into and subdued the Semien, a high mountain region of snow and ice, to which his successor Asbaha (514–42) was wont to deport those whom he had sentenced to banishment.

against whom he sent a powerful expedition under his brothers Shaizan and Hadefa, overpowering six of their kings and all their people. Remembering that the kings of Axum spoke always of their exploits in the language of extreme grandiloquence the 'kings' were quite probably no more than chiefs of sub-tribes, nor is it known who they were, or how far the punitive raid had penetrated. He appears, however, to have settled the Beja problem of his day by moving some four or five thousand of them to new settlements in the district of Matlia, probably more closely under his control, providing them with food, clothing and animals, a solution which would have found favour with the governor of Kassala who, in 1910, considered that the only way of dealing with the Hadendowa was to move them en masse to Kordofan. 'We compelled them to change their abode, and sent them to a place of our country called M...a',[1] and in thankfulness for his victory the king dedicated statues of gold, silver and brass to his gods.

Aizanas seems to have been dowered with much of the megalomania and military ability of his greater predecessor in another sphere, Alexander of Macedon. His armies, recruited district by district on feudal lines, were well drilled and equally well handled, and then as now the southern Beja, though of their own initiative incapable of concerted effort, could be formidable if disciplined and well led. He appears to have lived for glory and conquest, and not content with subduing the Beja he harried the country of Afan, and finally (356) launched a great expedition down the Atbara against the Kasu and Nuba[2] who had plundered his subjects and maltreated his envoys:

And I rose in the might of the Lord of the Land, and I fought with them on the Takazzé, at the ford of Kamalké. Thereupon they took

---

[1] Salt, *A Voyage to Abysinnia, 1809–10* (1814), pp. 411–12.

[2] These were a race of dark-skinned Nuba from the south who, it has been suggested, had only recently occupied the greater part of the Meroitic kingdom, and are not the same people as the Red Nuba mentioned by Aizanas as living some way farther downstream, and who were quite possibly those whom Diocletian had subsidized in the Nile valley some three-quarters of a century before. (See Chapter VI.)

flight and would not stand against me. I followed them for three days, killing some and making others prisoner.... I set up my throne in that country within the confluence of the Seda and Takazzé.

It should be noted that Aizanas had by this time been converted to Christianity. It is related that Frumentius, a Syrian, was kidnapped with his brother from a ship near Adulis, and conveyed to Axum, where he became a protégé of the king. In due course he succeeded in converting him, probably about 340, and was later appointed bishop of Axum by Athanasius. His influence with Aizanas was great, and when he died Frumentius became regent of the kingdom during the minority of his son. It was to Aizanas also that the Emperor Constantine II (337–61) wrote concernedly on the question of heresy, and advising that Frumentius should be replaced by someone more orthodox. Thus came Christianity to Abyssinia, and although it was to die out eventually among the tribes who later came under Mohammedan domination, it gained a much closer hold, and exercised a much more profound influence than among the northern Beja, whose acceptance of Christianity some two centuries later was both superficial and transitory.

At the height of its power the kingdom continued to have contact with the outside world, and its alliance was sought both for commercial and military reasons. Its fleet, based on Adulis, was engaged actively in the carrying trade of the Red Sea, though to nothing like the same extent as those of Arabia, and though Rome was jealous of the traffic, she found it desirable to maintain friendly relations. Negotiations with Axum are first mentioned in the reign of Aurelian (270–5), possibly in connection with joint action to be taken against the northern Beja who had then occupied part of Upper Egypt. Later, about 337, Constantine I negotiated a commercial treaty, using Frumentius as his envoy, and the preoccupation of Constantine II with orthodoxy and his representations to Axum have already been mentioned.

It is alleged that gold was for long unknown or unobtainable in the kingdom, so that brass and copper were used for coinage, and such gold as the king was able to acquire was obtained by barter from a primitive and shy people, the Sasou, who lived in the frankincense country to the south, to which every two years an expedition was sent from Axum to exchange meat, iron and salt for gold. 'The country known as Sasou', says Cosmas, 'is itself near the ocean, just as the ocean is near the frankincense country in which there are many gold mines.'[1] Such expeditions were six months on the road, and the caravans which composed them travelled heavily armed. Copper coins were in frequent use, and many specimens are still to be discovered today. The later kings coined gold, and also used it lavishly for ornamentation and display.

When the Emperor Justin I (518–28) sent an embassy under Nonnus to Axum to invite participation in the war against Persia the kingdom was still powerful and warlike, though the king, Asbaha (514–42), pleaded that he had no ships and borrowed sixty from Justin. But the seeds of decay had already set in, and retrogression in culture is illustrated by the fact that Asbaha, unlike so many of his predecessors, knew no Greek, that inscriptions were no longer written in that language, and that the coinage, while reproducing Greek symbols and wording, did so in base and corrupt form. Nevertheless, Nonnus reports that Axum was still a centre of trade in spices, hides, gold dust and ivory, and the mission of which he was head had been inspired by Asbaha's successful invasion of the Yemen in 525.

Dhu Nuwwas, the last of the Himyarite kings of the Yemen, had Jewish sympathies and was a notable persecutor of Christians. Asbaha of Axum, who is alleged later to have become a monk, was an equally fanatical Christian, and the expedition which he equipped for the relief of his co-religionists in the Yemen was brilliantly successful.[2] Dhu Nuwwas was

---

[1] *Christian Topography*, p. 52.

[2] Milne (*A History of Egypt under Roman Rule* (1924), p. 108) is of the opinion that their quarrel 'arose out of the Indian trade in which both nations had a considerable interest'. The expedition must be classed as a raid only, and of no lasting significance.

killed, and the Yemen became a dependency of Axum with a governor appointed by the king. Persia at that time was threatening both the Roman Empire from the east, and Southern Arabia from the north, a fact which no doubt inspired the Roman request for an alliance with a power which, however, was already past its zenith and unable much longer to be of any assistance. The military effort which Axum put forth in the conquest of the Yemen did in fact so exhaust her that she never again recovered her former strength, and the new dependencies of Himyar and the Yemen were to be a constant source of discord and trouble.

To this period belong the exploits of Abraha, often described as a king of Axum, though he was never in fact any such thing. In 531 civil war broke out in Southern Arabia between Ariat, governor of the Himyar, and Abraha, governor of the Yemen, in which the former enjoyed the benefit of royal support. It brought him no advantage, however, because his rival had him murdered, and assumed the title of king of Himyar which, after a futile campaign to unseat him, Asbaha eventually acknowledged. The fact that he also called himself king of Axum has led to confusion and assumption by some authorities that Asbaha was Abraha, or that the kingdom was ruled by two kings jointly. Abraha's career is of particular interest on account of his expedition against Mecca in 570 which is mentioned in the Quran as the 'Battle of the Elephant'.[1] The town of Saphar was at that time the seat of a bishopric, the church of which was desecrated by Arabs of the Qureish, and in revenge Abraha marched against Mecca, the site of the sacred stone later to be famous as the Ka'aba, with thirteen elephants and a large army. He failed on the verge of success when his army was smitten by smallpox and retired in disorder.

About 560 the Emperor Justinian sent yet another embassy

---

[1] 'Have ye not seen what the Lord hath done against the People of the Elephant, how He hath frustrated their designs and led them astray? For He sent against them the birds of the air to discomfit them with pellets of earth, so that they became as the harvest which is green before the locust.'

to Axum under Julian, to enquire into the possibility of diverting the silk trade from Persia to a new route through the Red Sea, but Gabra Maskal, a son of Asbaha, professed himself helpless through lack of ships. Julian describes the barbaric splendour of the king, who appeared half-naked, but decked with gold ornaments, and riding in a chariot drawn by four elephants.

Almost the last of the kings of Axum known to history was Armah, who gave sanctuary to followers of Mohammed who had fled from Mecca and Medina between 615 and 629, when the end of the kingdom was already near. Adulis was destroyed by Arab raiders about 640. The northern Beja on the Atbara, finding nothing to restrain them, began to infiltrate into Tigré and Hamasien, and the kingdom, exhausted, enfeebled and disrupted, entered its final decline. The Moslem invasion of Egypt in 641 cut its only remaining line of communication with the outside world, and ruined its trade, and at some time in the ninth century the last of its princelings was displaced by a Shoan chief, and the name of Axum is heard no more.

It left behind it as evidence of its one-time greatness a series of unique and incredible monuments, its language, which is still that of the Ethiopian scriptures, three varieties of which are spoken still by the Amhara, by the plateau tribes of Eritrea, and by the now Moslem southern Beja, and lastly a few incomplete and tantalizingly fragmentary inscriptions. More than this, it left behind it the traditional and habitual respect for authority which today is one of the most characteristic traits of the southern Beja, and which later was to cause them to accept with meekness the feudal domination of a number of small superior non-Beja castes.

KINGS OF AXUM FOR WHOM THERE
IS HISTORICAL WARRANT

Of the kings of Axum who are known to us from their inscriptions, their coinage, or for other reasons, only a few are identifiable. They are:

(1) Zoscales, *c.* A.D. 76–99. Mentioned by the writer of the *Periplus*, and identified as the Za Hakal of some of the lists of kings. Was possibly the second of the dynasty.

(2) Aphilas of Demel. Date unknown, but may be the king whose inscription was found on the Monumentum Adulitanum. *c.* 275 (Kammerer, *op. cit.* p. 155.)

(3) Ousanas of Guissé. Known from his coinage. A pagan.

(4) Sembruthes. Known from a fragmentary inscription.

(5) Endybis. Known from his coinage. A pagan.

(6) Ela Amida of Halen, 314–25. The father of Aizanas, known from inscriptions, his own and his son's.

(7) Aizanas of Halen, *c.* 325–70. The greatest of the kings of Axum. His principal feat of arms was the overthrow of Meroë in 356. Became a Christian.

(8) Asbaha, 514–42. Also known as Caleb. Overthrew Dhu Nuwwas, king of the Yemen. Believed to have ended his days as a monk.

(9) Beta Israel, 542–50. Son of Asbaha. Known from his coinage.

(10) Gabra Maskal. Second son of Asbaha. 550–64 or 570.

(11) Armah, *c.* 610–35. Gave asylum to persecuted followers of Mohammed, and later corresponded with him.

CHAPTER VI

THE ENEMIES OF ROME
(50 B.C.–A.D. 640)

The Blemminges which carried bows and arrowes made of dragons
bones.   ELIZABETHAN TRANSLATION OF HELIODORUS

Augustus, after he had defeated Antony and Cleopatra at
Actium in 30 B.C., and annexed Egypt as a province of the
Roman Empire, thought it of sufficient importance to station
three legions there. These were later reduced to one, which
remained encamped close to Alexandria to overawe the populace
of that turbulent city, and the defence of the frontier was left
to auxiliaries and local levies, reinforced in times of trouble by
regular troops. Syene (Assuan) became the garrison town for
the defence of Egypt against the Nuba and the Beja, but posts
were maintained also in the Dodekaschoinus, the Land of the
Twelve Schoinoi, which contained Talmis (Kalabsha) and
eight other towns, the most southerly of which was Hierosycaminos (Maharaka), and the Romans also recruited and
trained a camel corps, the *ala dromedarorum*, for scouting
operations in the desert against the Beja.

As early as 23 B.C. there was trouble on the southern frontier,
and an expedition under Gaius Petronius destroyed Napata in
retaliation for Nubian raids on Syene. Of the Beja there is but
yet little mention, and it was not until about the middle of the
third century that they became a serious menace, and from their
occupied cities in the Nile valley threatened to upset Roman
control of the Thebaid. Then as now they consisted of a number
of different tribes, not under one chief, but several, and it is
probable that those whom classical writers knew as the
Blemmyes were those sections which lived closest to the Nile,
and were rather more sedentary and slightly more civilized
than the purely nomadic sections in the desert and on the Red
Sea coast. Strabo speaks of several different peoples inhabiting

Map 2. The Nile Valley and Red Sea in classical times

that area, the Blemmyes and the Megabari of the Nile valley and the skirts of the Thebaid, and the Fish-Eaters and Troglodytes of the sea coast south of Berenice. Who the Megabari were is not certain, but it is probable that, like the Blemmyes, they were a Beja tribe, slightly less primitive than some, but essentially the same people, and of similar habits and characteristics.[1] Some observers have been at pains to conclude that the Blemmyes in particular, by reason of a superior culture and sedentary habits, are not to be connected with the Beja nomads of the Eastern Desert: 'the ethnological theory which connects them [the Blemmyes] with a race so hostile to culture as the Beja is a mere theory at present undemonstrated.'[2]

The conclusion is, I think, a false one. There is little evidence that the Blemmyes possessed more than the merest smattering of culture derived from their subject peoples, and while it can be accepted that for some considerable period from about A.D. 200 onwards they settled in or close to the Nile valley, I do not believe (from my knowledge of modern Beja settlements) that they were ever townspeople, or that their settlement came to much more than a partial occupation of inhabited or previously inhabited sites, and as dwellers in other men's houses.

It is true that the excavators of Karanog (Woolley and McIver) speak of a Blemmyan period in connection with this occupation, which in their opinion lasted for some four hundred and fifty years, and also of Blemmyan culture, architecture, pottery and furnishings. Such a description is misleading. The excavations at Karanog revealed traces of 'a pastoral people... a mixed folk headed by a non-negroid aristocracy; they shared the civilization and, in most points at least, the religion of the Meroitic Empire',[3] and the only justification for alluding to the essentially Meroitic culture of this predominantly negroid people as Blemmyan is that the Blemmyes subjugated and

---

[1] The Blemmyes, and other related tribes, are mentioned by nearly all writers from Herodotus (c. 450 B.C.) to Olympiodorus (c. A.D. 425).

[2] Crowfoot, 'The Island of Meroe', *Arch. Survey of Egypt* (1911), p. 35.

[3] Woolley and McIver, *Karanog, The Romano-Nubian Cemetery* (1910), p. 6.

occupied that part of the Nile valley for some hundreds of years in the role of a small but dominant aristocracy. That they themselves contributed anything to the civilization which they found there is open to doubt, and there is, on the contrary, evidence of the debasing character of their influence, pointing to the domination of a fairly highly-cultured subject people by a primitive and barbaric race of primarily nomadic habits, to whom can be attributed the general deterioration which had set in before the final defeat and expulsion of the Blemmyes c. 540. We find the Meroitic script in general use, and a culture that, so far as comparison is yet possible, corresponds with that of Meroë, though its rougher style bears witness to its provincial character. We find lastly marks of a cattle-keeping people, who were at the same time apparently huntsmen and warriors, fitted as beseems a desert folk, with the bullock's hide armour and light missile weapons that Dio Cassius ascribes to the Blemmyes.[1]

The Blemmyes seem to have remained, even to the very end, essentially a desert and nomadic people, and I agree with Kirwan that 'the name Blemmyes was applied by writers of the Roman period to a collection of nomad tribes scattered about the Eastern Desert between Abyssinia, Egypt and the Red Sea; a people frequently on the move, like the modern Beja tribes, whose geographical limits are the same',[2] and he remarks elsewhere that their wide distribution, their numerous tribal divisions, and their nomadic habits, all go far to explain the inconsistencies of classical historians and writers.[3]

It has been suggested also that the Blemmyes were not Beja for the reason that they were a camel-owning people, whereas the latter are predominantly cattle owners.[4] In actual fact the Beja are, and always have been, owners and breeders of both, but as for many hundreds of years now cattle have been unable to survive in any great numbers north of the present Port Sudan-

[1] *Ibid.* p. 89.
[2] Kirwan, *Oxford University Excavations at Firka* (1939), p. 48.
[3] 'Studies in the Later History of Nubia', *Liverpool Annals*, vol. XXIV, p. 74.
[4] Robinson, 'Desiccation or Destruction', *S.N.R.* vol. XVIII (1) (1935), p. 129.

Atbara railway line, it is not surprising that the Blemmyes, who were one of the most northern of the Beja tribes, should have had but few cattle, or should have bred camels even as the Besharin do in much the same latitudes today. I am even more inclined to believe, therefore, that all the peoples of the Eastern Desert were then as now ethnologically of one stock, and that as the Beja of today consist of many tribes, Hadendowa, Beni Amer and others, so they did then, counting among their numbers the primitive Ichthyophagi at one end of the cultural scale, and the more sophisticated Blemmyes at the other.

The rock-pictures of the Eastern Desert which can be ascribed to the Blemmyes tell us little about them, other than that they were mainly a camel-owning people, whose weapons were the bow and spear, who used both pagan and Christian symbols, and whose drawings, animals apart, represent quite other than the everyday things of their desert existence. It is my experience of primitive peoples of artistic bent, such as the Shilluk and modern Nuba, that except for animals they tend to depict those things which to them are strange and out of the ordinary. Thus their drawings are full of representations of motor-cars, aeroplanes, and Nile steamers, and of a peculiar helmeted race who sit on chairs and use firearms. In this the Beja of the Blemmyan period were no different. Their drawings are of men wearing shirt-like garments and Phrygian caps, and armed with swords and rectangular shields.[1] Whatever they are meant to be they are not Beja: the clothes, the swords, the shape of the shields, and the fact that some of the figures depicted are horsemen, are all evidence of that. My guess is that they may be pictures of Roman soldiers, or possibly of Greek mercenaries employed in Ptolemaic times to garrison the mines and the Red Sea trading stations. To this period also (c. A.D. 100) belongs the legend of an invasion of the Atbai by Abu el Malik ibn Shamnar-Yerash, king of the Yemen, who perished with his whole army in an attempt to seize the emerald mines of the

[1] Winkler, *Rock Drawings of Southern Upper Egypt* (1938), vol. II, Plates V and VI.

Eastern Desert. Such contemporary records as exist make no mention of it, and the tale survives only in the chronicles of a few later Arab historians.

Rome was not interested in gold, so that the desert mines remained unworked, and as regards trade her interest was focused to the south on the entrepôts of the Far East trade at Aden and the southern gates of the Red Sea. She had no reason, therefore, to disturb the Beja other than occasionally, as for instance in A.D. 137, when the generals of Hadrian, cutting a road from the newly founded city of Antinioöpolis to the port of Berenice, found it necessary to chastise the desert tribes (the Agriophagi) who objected to it. Peace of a sort seems to have been maintained until 249 when the Beja attacked Upper Egypt in force in the reign of the Emperor Decius and were with difficulty repelled. In 268 they came on again in strange alliance with the Palmyreans who had invaded Egypt with an army of 70,000 men and on retiring left a garrison of 5000 to make head against the Romans with the help of local patriots and of the Blemmyes. For the whole of the reign of Aurelian (270–5) Upper Egypt was in turmoil. The Beja overran and occupied a number of towns in the Thebaid, where they remained until forced out by Probus in 276. Even so they continued to raid as far downstream as Ptolemais, and it was not until about 280 that Probus, by then himself Emperor, succeeded finally in driving them back into their deserts, and in establishing the frontier once again at Hierosycaminos.

It was a temporary check only, and in 284 the Emperor Diocletian deemed it expedient to abandon the Dodeka-schoinus, where he formed a buffer state of Nuba to prevent it falling into Beja hands, strengthening their occupation with monetary aid, and paying the Beja a subsidy to cease from raiding.[1] It had little effect, and the garrison at Syene could only look on helplessly while the Beja devastated the Thebaid.

[1] Nuba relations with the Beja were uncertain. They were often at war, but in 450 they combined to attack the Roman power in Egypt. The authority is Procopius, *De Bello Persico*, I, xix.

Rome was in decline, and although Beja appeared in the triumphs both of Probus and of Diocletian, and excited much astonishment by their appearance, there was little that the Roman garrisons could do to stop them.[1] For two centuries or more they dominated the Southern Thebaid and made their name a

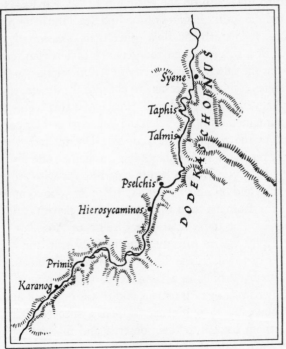

Map 3. The Southern Thebaid

terror to the peoples of the Nile valley far beyond it. There is record also of a fourth-century raid by Beja on Raithe (Tor) on the opposite shores of the Red Sea. They appear to have captured a boat and to have compelled its crew to sail it for them, but after sacking Raithe and putting many of its inhabitants to the sword, they were themselves annihilated by the local tribesmen.

[1] 'Blemmys etiam subegi quorum captivos Roma transmisit, qui mirabilem sui visum stupenite populo Romano praebuerunt' (Vospicius, *Vita Probi*, xvii).

Gibbon has remarked on their temerity in daring to match themselves with Rome: 'these barbarians whom antiquity, shocked by the deformity of their figure, has almost excluded from the human species, presumed to rank themselves among the enemies of Rome'.[1] But inferiority is the last thing those desert warriors were likely to feel, and it is clear that as a fighting race they incurred respect. They are described by all as ferocious and untamable, expert bowmen and spearmen, adepts at dealing with cavalry by diving between the horses' legs and disembowelling them, deadly fighters with all the short-lived but desperate valour of Hamitic peoples, ruthless in the exploitation of victory, so that nothing lived beneath their spears, sullen, obstinate, and intractable in defeat. They were believed also to drink the blood of their enemies, particularly of those killed in pursuance of a blood feud, and as late as 1814 Burckhardt relates that this savage custom still lingered on among the Halenga at Kassala.

They worshipped a strange galaxy of gods, some Egyptian, some Sabaean, and some peculiarly their own, and were said to offer sacrifices to the sun. 'A barbarous people', says Mommsen, 'of revolting savageness...who had not abandoned human sacrifices.'[2] Of any organized form of government they knew nothing, each group owing allegiance only to its own chief, often at war among themselves, but ready as ever to unite under an outstanding leader for a major raid against their neighbours. Their occupation of the Nile valley was probably at its most permanent in the century immediately preceding their ultimate expulsion. They appear to have united to form a petty kingship, and to have had some pretensions to a settled existence and an orderly form of government. Olympiodorus, who visited Syene about 423, met there the phylarchs of the Blemmyes, and accompanied them on a visit to their cities of Phoinikon, Chiris, Taphis, Talmis and Primis, which latter he says was the most

---

[1] *The Decline and Fall of the Roman Empire*, vol. VI, p. 138.
[2] *The Provinces of the Roman Empire*, vol. II (1909). (See Chapter XIII for the Beja.)

southern of their settlements, and he was also allowed to visit the emerald mines in the desert by permission of their king. The Blemmyes, while uninterested in gold, seem to have maintained control of the emerald mines, and to have supplied Abyssinia for trade with India.

In 429 the Beja tribes combined in a spectacular raid against the Great Oasis, plundered it effectively, and carried off large numbers of the inhabitants as slaves. In 450, however, the power of Rome in Upper Egypt was re-asserted. Maximinus, the general of the Emperor Marcian (450–7), drove them south, defeated them decisively, and in 451 concluded a treaty with them by which they restored all captives (the victims of the Oasis raid), gave hostages and paid tribute, but were allowed to remove the image of Isis from her sanctuary at Philae for worship in the desert.[1] Maximinus not only defeated the Beja but appears to have been successful in the much more difficult task of winning their confidence and respect. In their negotiations with him they at first proposed a truce for as long as he was in Egypt, then for his lifetime, and having finally signed an agreement to keep the peace for a hundred years, raided the Thebaid and rescued their hostages as soon as they heard of his death. Thereafter, for the remainder of the fifth century and part of the sixth they remained in occupation of the Southern Thebaid between Assuan and Primis, subsidized by Rome, lording it over a subservient riverain population, and carrying on a desultory war with the Nuba to the south of them.

Shortly before the middle of the sixth century there occurred two events of major importance—their decisive defeat and expulsion from the Nile valley by the Nuba, and their partial conversion to Christianity. Of their war with the Nuba little is known, but certain it is that in the third or fourth decade of

---

[1] They were also devotees of the god Mandulis, Lord of Talmis, 'very great among the deserts', for whom the Romans built a temple at Talmis (Kalabsha). (See Kirwan, *Oxford University Excavations at Firka*, p. 47.) Mandulis was very possibly the Beja conception of Mithras, and Min, also a popular god in the desert, seems to have been Apollo, the Thunder God.

the sixth century when they were heavily defeated by the Nuba
king, Silko, they were in most things pagan still, because in the
famous inscription in the temple of Mandulis at Talmis in which
the king celebrated his victory, he makes mention of their idols:

I came to Talmis and Taphis and twice I fought with the Blemmyes,
and God gave me the victory once and thrice again.... I conquered
them and made myself master of their cities... and they made
supplication to me, and I made peace with them, and they swore to
me by their idols. I trusted in their oaths that they were honourable
men. Then I returned to my own country.

When I became King I did not follow after other Kings, but went
before them. As for those who strive against me I do not permit
them to survive, unless they respect me and do me homage, for I am
as a lion in the plains and as an oryx in the mountains.

I fought with the Blemmyes from Ibrim to (Primis) to Talmis
once and for all, and I ravaged the lands of those south of the Nuba
who sought to stand against me. The chiefs of the nations who fought
against me I do not permit to sit in the shade, but outside in the sun:
nor to drink water in their own houses, and I carry off the women
and children of those who resist me.[1]

Woolley is of the opinion that Silko fought two campaigns
at least against the Blemmyes, one shortly after his conversion
to Christianity (c. 530–40), and another later one in alliance
with the Romans after the Blemmyes had risen in revolt against
Justinian's destruction of their gods at Philae. The inscription
at Talmis can be so interpreted, and there is evidence of frequent Blemmyan raids into Egypt in 538–9. That they were
inspired by Justinian's closure of the temple at Philae is a moot
point, and it is equally possible that he closed the temple as a
preventive measure.

Whatever the circumstances, the king's victory was both
complete and decisive, and from now on the power of the Beja
was on the wane. They were expelled from their settlements in

---

[1] I have seen several variants of this inscription of which the above is a
composite version. The picture of the defeated chieftains sitting com-
plainingly in the sun is not without humour.

the Nile valley, and from the moment of their withdrawal into the eastern deserts the name of Blemmyes is rarely heard again. Procopius, writing in 543, makes no mention of them in his description of the tribes about Assuan or in the Dodeka-schoinus, but they were still raiding Philae as late as 577 in the course of a revolt in alliance with the Nuba which was crushed by Aristomachus, governor of Egypt under Tiberius II.

Of the conversion of the Beja to Christianity very little also is known. In 536, or thereabouts, the Emperor Justinian closed the temple of Isis at Philae and rededicated it to Christian worship, his emissaries removing the statues of the gods, and imprisoning the priests who served them. This policy, inspired by a desire to break up a rallying point of the desert tribes on the southern frontier, was a mistake, as it removed the one object in Roman territory for which the Beja had respect, and they reacted to the removal by renewal of their raids. About this time also Monophysite Christianity was introduced into Nubia by Julian, the emissary of the Empress Theodora, in the teeth of opposition from her husband, and this mission was followed by another headed by Longinus in 570. These missions had considerable success in Nubia, and possibly also with some of the less remote Beja, but it does not seem that Christianity went more than skin deep, or became more than a matter of outward form. Up to the time of their conversion to Islam some five hundred years later their beliefs remained a peculiar mixture of paganism, sun- and stone-worship, venera-tion of Isis, Serapis and Mandulis, with a thin overlay of Jacobite Christianity, and as the influence of Rome declined the Beja relapsed into the various forms of idolatry which they may not even nominally have abandoned.[1]

Henceforward, until the appearance of the Arabs in the seventh century, and even later, the Beja have no recorded history. As far as is known the southern frontiers of Egypt,

---

[1] The Jacobites were Monophysites who believed only in one nature of God. They were so called from the monk Jagoub el Baradai, who framed the final canon of their belief.

so frequently ravaged in the past, remained inviolate, and the inhabitants enjoyed a welcome respite from incursions from the desert. It can only be assumed that their defeat by the Nuba was in fact a major disaster which crippled them effectively as a fighting power for some time to come, and threw them into an anarchic period of dissension and civil war. Thus they were to remain until the rediscovery of the gold-mines drew upon them the attentions of the Arab conquerors of Egypt.

CHAPTER VII

THE ARAB INFILTRATION
(640–1520)

Some parcel of the soil of Arabia smelling of Samn
and camels.   DOUGHTY

At some time in the seventh century A.D. there began a slow
and by no means continuous process of infiltration by Arab
tribes, never at any time of great proportions, yet sufficiently
pronounced as to result eventually in all the Beja peoples
becoming Moslem. The earliest arrivals were not however
Moslems, and are said to have been a fragment of a Himyarite
tribe which came by way of the Red Sea from Shihr in Southern
Arabia and settled among the Beja of the Atbai and Sinkat hills,
intermarrying with them, and acquiring predominance partly
by virtue of superior culture, and partly by reason of the matrilinear system of succession in vogue among them:

With them the son by the daughter, or son by the sister succeeds to
property, to the exclusion of the true son, and they allege that the
birth of the daughter's or sister's son is more certain, because at all
events, whether it is the husband or someone else who is the father,
he is always her son.[1]

Their arrival prior to the Hegira is well established, for they
are later spoken of as Jacobite Christians who were converted
to Islam only after the appearance of Arab invaders from Egypt
in the ninth century. These immigrants, to give them the name
by which they were most commonly known by Arab writers
and travellers, were the Hadareb, a Beja corruption of Hadarma,
or inhabitants of the Hadramaut. To the Beja, however, they
were as commonly known as the Bellou by reason of the fact

[1] Burckhardt, *Travels in Nubia* (1822), p. 458. Burckhardt in all references
to the medieval Beja is quoting in translation from Makrizi, a painstaking but
not always critical writer, who himself draws largely on the now lost 'Nubia,
Mukurra, Alwa, the Beja, and the Nile' of Ibn Selim el Assuani, who was sent
on a mission to Nubia in the reign of the Caliph Mu'izz *c.* 970.

that on arrival they spoke a strange tongue, the Beja for which (as it still is) was Bellaweit, though it was not until they had been driven south from the Atbai in the fifteenth century that the latter name replaced the former in common usage. Thus, though they are indeed one and the same people, the use of two different names at different times has given rise to confusion and assumption that they were two, a confusion which, however, never existed in local minds. 'It is well known', says the Amarar historian, 'that the Bellawiyun are Arabs who came from Arabia before the main immigration of the Arabs to the Sudan, and dwelt in the Beja and mingled with them.'[1]

Most writers have been content to classify them as Beja which, in some sense, after centuries of intermarriage with genuine Beja tribes they indeed became, the Himyarite strain in their blood gradually disappearing. Described variously as Belo, Ballaw, and Balau, sections have been traced as far south as Harar, and they have been identified, wrongly, with the Kelou, an autochthonous Beja tribe at one time living in the Gash and Baraka valleys, and also as a Beja tribe from the Tigrean plateau with Abyssinian connections, which drifted to the western lowlands some time in the fourteenth century. Longrigg yet again states: 'that these (the Belu) were of Beja origin is certain; that they entered Eritrea as pagans and soon (at the latest by the Fifteenth Century) adopted Islam on the coast, and Christianity elsewhere, not less so'.[2]

This description is not altogether accurate. It is not improbable, as Rossini believes, that there were at least two groups of Bellou, a northern one, the Hadareb of the Atbai and the Sinkat hills, and a southern one, which was the nucleus of the Bellou kingdom which flourished between the latitudes of Suakin and Massawa from how early on is not known, and whose fortunes will be traced in a later chapter.[3] Kirwan (*A.A.A.*, vol. XXIV, pp. 74–5) advances the theory that the name Bellou derives from Blemmyes. This is demonstrably untrue

---

[1] Sudan Government Archives. [2] *A Short History of Eritrea* (1945), p. 32.
[3] Munziger dates the rise of this kingdom as about 1370.

in that the Bellou were Himyarites who emigrated from Southern Arabia in the sixth century A.D. and could therefore have had no previous connection with the Hamitic Beja. Idrisi, who infers that they had something to do with the Rum (Greeks ?), is obviously mistaken and confused by the fact of their Jacobite Christianity. Munziger says that they came from the north in the fifteenth century. So far as the history of what is now Eritrea is concerned that is correct, for it was about this time that they were driven south from the Atbai and then from the Sinkat area. Crawford rightly attributes to them an Arabian origin, but, failing to connect them with the Hadareb, dates their arrival some eight centuries too late.[1] The trail is confused because at different times in their history they have been given different names by different peoples, the Abyssinians even going so far as to apply the name to such tribes as the Dabainya and Shukria who had no connection with the Bellou whatsoever.

It is necessary also to distinguish between the medieval Hadareb (the Bellou) and their modern counterparts so un- flatteringly described by nineteenth-century visitors to the Sudan, mainly Arteiga, Ashraf and others, who by then were very predominantly Beja by blood, but including also large numbers of half-caste Beja, the result of intermarriage with Turks, Egyptians, Circassians, Bosnians, etc., all the rag-tag and bobtail of the Middle East who sought to profit by the slave traffic and other more legitimate trade of the Sudan after the Turkish occupation of Suakin. The Arteiga strain pre- dominated, and their chief was the Emir el Hadarba who shared the revenues of the port, first with its Turkish, and later with its Egyptian governors. Osman Digna was a not untypical product of Hadareb society. His ancestors were Kurds who had settled in Suakin in the sixteenth century, and there followed three centuries of intermarriage with local women, Osman's own mother being of the Bushariab/Hadendowa.

It would appear from the little that is known of them at this period that the Hadareb cannot have arrived in any great

[1] *The Fung Kingdom of Sennar* (1950), pp. 111–12.

number for although they acquired the status of a ruling caste, they failed to establish their own language and, from being idolators, imitated the Beja in adopting a form of Christianity. Their Arabian origin manifests itself in their possession of horses, animals which the Beja at all times have very heartily disliked, and Idrisi, the only Arab writer of the time to speak of them as Bellou, and not Hadareb, says: 'The neighbourhood of Assuan is invaded by black horsemen called Belliyun, and it is claimed that they have been Christians since the time of the Egyptians. They wander in the desert between the Beja and the Habash, and come as far as Nubia.'

In 641 the Arab armies under 'Amr ibn el 'Asi overran Egypt and pushed south into Dongola, and there arises thence the unsubstantiated account of a Beja kinglet called Shih or Souh, whose capital was on the river Atbara, who marched in alliance with the king of the Nuba to the relief of the Roman garrison of Oxyrhynchus (Bahnasa) and was there heavily defeated despite an army of 50,000 men and several elephants.[1] Bahnasa is, however, a long way, an almost impossibly long way, for a Beja army to march, and it is more probable that the story relates to the battle near Debba in Dongola in which Khalid ibn Waleed, 'the Sword of God', defeated a Nubian army reinforced by Beja in about 651.

Thereafter the Beja had little further contact with the Arabs until Ebeidallah ibn Hadhab, who was then governor of Upper Egypt, made a treaty with them (one suspects that they had been raiding as usual, and had been repulsed)[2] by which they agreed to pay tribute of 300 young camels, to give no asylum to escaped slaves, and to grant toleration and safety to all Moslems within their territories. From this it seems probable that the Arabs had already begun exploitation of the gold and emerald mines of the Eastern Desert, and it does not appear,

[1] Burckhardt, op. cit. p. 482.
[2] 'During Islam, and before that time they (the Beja) had oppressed the eastern banks of Upper Egypt and had ruined many villages' (Burckhardt, op. cit. p. 460).

treaty or no, that the Beja felt at all kindly towards their intrusion.[1] Their raids into the Nile valley were frequent, and in 831 the Caliph Mamoun, grandson of Haroun el Rashid, sent an expedition against them under Abdullah ibn Jiham. As a result the original treaty was re-affirmed and amplified, and by agreement of a Beja chief whose name is Arabicized as Kanun Abdel Aziz, tribute was re-assessed at 100 camels or 300 *dinars*. Moslems were promised protection for property, mosques, and religion, no assistance was to be given to their enemies, hostages were handed over, and the dominion of the caliph was recognized from Assuan to Dahlak.

Within twenty years of the signing of this treaty the Beja rose again against Egypt. In 854 under a chief called Olbab (or Ali Baba) they massacred the Arab inhabitants of the mines, slave and free, refused tribute, and raided as far north as Esna with devastating effect. Ansaba ibn Ishak, the last of the Arab governors of Egypt, sent against them a carefully prepared expedition under Mohammed Abdullah ibn Gami'. Supplies in six transports were sent by sea to Sanga, near Aidhab, and Ibn Gami' marched from Kus with a picked force of 7000 men.[2] The Beja adopted Fabian tactics in the hope that their opponents might first be weakened by thirst and hunger, but were forced to give battle to prevent them from reaching the coast and their supplies; some of these supplies must have been landed much farther north than Aidhab, as the battle took place near Jebel Zabara. The Beja army consisted of spearman mounted on

[1] The earliest evidence of Moslem Arab settlement among the Beja comes from a tombstone at Nubt, some eighty miles north-east of Musmar, which is dated 149 A.H. (A.D. 766). This is some sixty-five years prior to Abdullah ibn Jiham's expedition, and it is not known why there should have been an Arab settlement in so isolated a spot, as there are no signs of gold workings: nor is it known whence the settlers had come. The latest date deciphered so far on a tombstone from Nubt is 927, which gives the settlement a life of well over 150 years.

[2] Ibn Khaldun (*El 'Ibar wa Diwan...Khabar*, pt. II, p. 277) says 20,000 men, but in view of the difficulty of maintaining a force of that size in the desert and the emphasis laid on smallness, I prefer the lesser figure. It was possibly even smaller.

PLATE III

WATERING CATTLE

camels which they handled with amazing dexterity, but Ibn
Gami' defeated them by a surprise attack in which the noise of
the bells fastened to his horses' necks upset the Beja camels and
stampeded them. He thus gained a complete victory, the terms
of Ibn Jiham's treaty were re-affirmed, and after giving hostages,
Olbab's nephew, who had succeeded him, was sent to Iraq
where he had audience with the Caliph Jaafer el Mitwakkil.

The historian Yagoubi, writing at the end of the ninth
century A.D., names six Beja kingdoms lying between Assuan
and Massawa:[1]

(1) Tankish, extending from Assuan to Khor Baraka, and inhabited by various tribes, Hadareb, Zenafig, Arbagda, and others.
In this kingdom were mines of gold, emeralds, and marble.

(2) Belgin, a land of many cities, inhabited by pagans who
were also magicians and plucked out their eye-lashes and front
incisor teeth.

(3) Bazin, bordering on Belgin and the Nubian kingdom of
Aloa.

(4) Jarin, extending from Badi' on the Red Sea to Khor
Baraka, and ruled by a powerful king.

(5) Qita'a, between Badi' and Feikun, very difficult of access.

(6) Nagash, whose capital Ka'bir was on the coast near
Dahlak, and whose inhabitants were merchants and Christians.

The only one of these which can be identified with certainty
is Tankish, with its population of Hadareb and their vassals,
the Zenafig, of whom Makrizi, writing much later, and quoting
Ibn Selim, states:

Among them [the Beja] are another race, the Zenafig, more numerous
than the Hadareb, but subject to them. They act as servants and
guards and supply them with cattle, and every chief of the Hadareb
has among his followers people of the Zenafig, who are as slaves
whom they inherit.[2]

[1] *Kitab el Buldan*, pt. I, pp. 218–19. The very frequent use by chroniclers
of the terms 'king' and 'kingdom' is misleading, and a truer picture emerges
if for 'king' we read 'chief', and for 'kingdom', 'district'.
[2] Burckhardt, *Travels in Nubia* (1822), p. 389.

This is clearly a description of the caste system brought with them from Arabia by the Hadareb, like the Sabaeans before them, and which in some parts was to survive until well into the twentieth century. The Hadareb were thus a ruling caste who, by reason no doubt of their Arab blood, were early converts to Islam (though Masudi remarks that they were very poor Moslems) whereas their serf tribes remained idolators, with some veneer of Christianity, until some time in the fourteenth century.

These were the tribes with whom the Arabs from Egypt had the closest contacts, and they are thus the best known to the Arab writers of the time. Of the other Beja tribes they remained largely ignorant, dependent on rumour and hearsay for their description, but Yagoubi's kingdoms of Belgin and Bazin were very probably inhabited by Beja resembling the Zenafig but not subject to the Hadareb, and may be those mentioned by Ibn Selim as speaking a language of their own and living a pastoral life in the deserts between the Nile and the sea. They were divided into numerous tribes and were pagans and devil-worshippers, much under the demoniac influences of their shamans. They lived in caves and tents of skins, their only food was the milk and flesh of their large herds of cattle and sheep, their weapons were spears, round bull-hide shields, and poisoned arrows. They had numerous herds of camels also, but it is their cattle which excite most admiration on account of their fine colour, long horns, and yield of milk. Hadjar, Dherbe, or Hejer, the Beja capital, was said by Yagoubi to be situated in the extremity of the island of the Beja, and has been placed by some authorities as far south as the angle between the Baraka and the Anseba. I do not think that this can be correct, as it was evidently not far from the Nile, lay in or near the gold country and on the route to Aidhab, and is said to have been largely inhabited by Hadarba.

Identification of the other kingdoms mentioned by Yagoubi is a matter of guesswork. The great king who ruled in Jarin may be an echo of the last glories of Axum, and Ka'bir, the capital of Nagash, might possibly be Adulis. According to Ibn Haukal (c. 997) a river called Dugn or Dujn flowed from the uplands of Tigré to lose itself in a heavily populated area west of the foothills. This can only be the Gash, and the Portuguese commentator, Paez, writing in the seventeenth century, refers to Deguin, an area inhabited by the Bellou, in which a river divides into many channels and then disappears, for which reason it is also known as Taka, the place of the dividing waters. Paez got his information at second hand from a Portuguese adventurer who accompanied the Viceroy of Tigré (the Bahr Nagash?) on an expedition to those parts. The river was also said to join the Takazze (Atbara) as the Gash may well have done at that time, and thence to flow to the Nile. There is a possible survival of the old name in the present village of Degein, which in To Bedawie means a firestone, i.e. a stone used for propping pots over a fire.

In the Atbai when Ibn Gami' finally returned to Egypt many of his army from the tribes of the Rabi'a and Guhayna chose to remain where they were, and the former succeeded eventually in making themselves masters of the mining country by a shrewd policy of alliance and intermarriage with the Beja, whose shamans are alleged to have advised them that such an alliance would bring them profit. Before the Rabi'a finally became supreme, however, there was a long and savage struggle with other Arab exploiters who were of similar ambitions, and who were not easily discomfited.

The mines were worked entirely by slave labour, by methods no better than those employed by the Pharaohs and the Ptolemies, and if anything the exploitation was harsher and more thorough. Emeralds appear to have been valued more highly than gold, and the output must have been considerable since, although the caliphs attempted repeatedly to increase their direct control of the mines but had to be content with a tithe of a third, or even as little as a fifth of the output, yet the wealth of the Fatimids and of their successors was prodigious. Gold, emeralds, topazes, turquoises and other precious stones found their way to Cairo in such quantities as to justify its description as the true city of the Thousand and One Nights, and it is recorded that a daughter of the Fatimid caliph Mu'izz (953–75), among a fortune for which 'four caliphs had successively sighed', left no less than five sacks of emeralds.[1]

There was thus every reason for the Arab adventurers who exploited the mines to fight among themselves, and in this the lead was given by a certain Abu Ommari Abdel Rahman, a descendant of the Caliph Omar, who re-opened the Wadi Allagi mines in 878 and succeeded in collecting so large an armed following that even the emir of Egypt, Ahmed ibn Tulun, was forced to treat him with respect. It is probable that the castles at Derheib in the Wadi Allagi were his strongholds, and he certainly used Aidhab as a port for the import of supplies from Egypt, with which Ibn Tulun attempted in vain to interfere. His followers came principally from the tribes of Mudr and Beni Tamin, but whereas he alienated even his own following by his revolting cruelties and oppressions, the Rabi'a, his greatest rivals, allied themselves with the local Beja and, after the most sanguinary of struggles, eventually defeated him. The end came when his brother was ambushed and killed by the Beja in the battle of Meisa when bringing supplies from Aidhab, and he himself, deserted by many of his followers, was murdered by one of the captains and his head sent to Ibn Tulun.

Thereafter the Rabi'a were supreme, and Masudi relates that in 940 Beshir ibn Marwan ibn Ishak, who was then their chief, had at his disposal a force of 3000 Arab cavalry and 30,000 Hadareb camelmen, once idolators but now Moslems, a generous and hospitable people, living under many chiefs, and in small family groups scattered through the hills and deserts, in all of which they were no different from what they always were, and are today.[2]

The Rabi'a, the Guhayna, and the Mudr were not, however,

[1] Lane-Poole, *A History of Egypt in the Middle Ages* (1901), pp. 111, 146.
[2] *Muruj el Dhahab*, vol. III, p. 33. The numbers are probably an exaggeration.

the only Arab settlers in the Beja country during this period. Towards the end of the seventh century a small group of the Hawazin crossed the Red Sea into Hamasien, where they acquired the name of Halenga, and whence they were later expelled by the enmity of the local inhabitants. By following the valley of the Mareb (the Gash) they eventually reached Taka and settled in the vicinity of the hill of To Lus (Kassala) and thus have the distinction of being the first Moslem Arabs to settle among the Beja. The tribes whom they found there have since disappeared, but there is reason to believe that at that time the Haffara and the Karabkinab were the principal tribes of the area. The Arteiga made their appearance somewhat later. Their ancestor, Ba Saffar, settled at Suakin about 800 and by marrying his sons to Beja wives became the progenitor of the kindred tribes of the Arteiga, Shaiab, and Hamran.

The Beja of the Atbai were to be brought into yet closer contact with the outer world from now on by the development of the small port of Aidhab as a pilgrim station and as a principal entrepôt for the Far East trade up the Red Sea to Egypt. It was by no means an ideal site, and all the necessities of life, even sweet water, had to be imported, yet it was first used as a port possibly in Ptolemaic times, and there is evidence of a developing trade in the tenth and eleventh centuries with India and China. Chinese ocean-going junks voyaged up the Red Sea with cargoes of spices such as cloves, cinnamon, and pepper, and the celadon of which fragments dating as early as a tenth-century Sung dynasty have been found at Aidhab. In return the Chinese shipped away dates, cotton, and sugar, and the highly prized edible sea-slugs for which the Red Sea is famous. The picture of the impassive and inscrutable Chinese doing business with the equally inscrutable Beja is a pleasant one: they must have been well matched, and it is a pity that no record of their dealings has survived. New prosperity was brought to Aidhab in the twelfth century by the closing of the overland pilgrim routes by the Crusaders of the Latin kingdom of Jerusalem. The port was thought to be beyond Christian reach (a miscalculation, as Renaud de Chatillon's galleys raided it in 1183),[1] and it developed despite its unpleasant climate and situation, on account of a deep-water roadstead close inshore, and the absence of offshore reefs.

The Beja were not slow to profit by this new prosperity. They conducted caravans through the desert to and from Kus, and made themselves responsible for local supplies such as milk, water, and firewood, and since they controlled the hinterland and could make trade impossible, they claimed successfully to share the port revenues with the governor appointed by the sultan of Egypt. Ibn Batuta, who visited it in 1326, reports that the king of the Beja (called El Hidirbi[2]) collected two-thirds of the imports through his agent, whereas the sultan received one-third only. Even so the persons and property of pilgrims were far from being safe. Many died of the hardships of the desert journey, in which they were often deliberately misled and robbed by their Beja guides, and in 1316, shortly before Ibn Batuta's visit, the ambassador of the Yemen and a large caravan of merchants were seized and plundered of all they had.

On arrival at Aidhab, the perils of the journey were by no means over. The passage of the Red Sea was accomplished in a day and a night in flimsy craft of which few of the Hadareb of Aidhab did not possess at least one, and which they crammed to over danger point with human freight, often with disastrous results. There is no single writer of the time who has not laid Aidhab under curse for its appalling climate, lack of amenities, and behaviour of its inhabitants, and yet the traffic went on, founded on man's lust for gain, and by contrast on the faith which will endure all things. Of the Hadareb who controlled it Makrizi says that they were as beasts, wild animals rather than men, and that the pilgrims who survived the rigours of the double passage and the desert journeys (and they were few) had the appearance of men but lately rescued from the grave,

[1] Newbold, 'The Crusaders in the Red Sea and the Sudan', *S.N.R.* vol. XXVI (2) (1945), p. 221.
[2] A title, not a name.

'and he who escapes reaches Aidhab as if risen out of his winding sheet, and entirely altered in features and body'.[1]

Ibn Batuta reports also the presence of Arabs of the Kawahla living among the Beja in the vicinity of Aidhab. These no doubt were the Kimmeilab who, by their own account, migrated there from Dongola in the thirteenth century, as the result of a blood feud. Unlike the Rabi'a and others they were interested in the pasturing of their flocks rather than in gold, and were expert horsemen who impressed the Beja by their skill in hunting down ostriches and other game. Their relationships with the local tribes were of the best, and when as the result of Islamization the Beja found it incumbent to provide themselves with an Arab ancestry, two of their tribes, the Amarar and the Besharin, chose to consider themselves as descended from Kahil.

The only other Arab groups of any importance to merge themselves with the Beja at this time were the Ashraf, who first appear in Suakin about 1350, and the Melhitkinab and Sigolab, who are reputed to be Bakaria and to have entered the Sudan with an expedition which the Sultan Nasir ibn Kala'oun sent against Nubia in 1289. When the army returned to Egypt they chose to remain and migrated to the Gash by way of the river Atbara.[2]

It is doubtful how far the sultans of Egypt exercised control over the country south and east of Assuan, and even in the ports of Aidhab and Suakin their authority seems constantly to have been in dispute, and by no means effective. As dynasty succeeded dynasty, and Ommayads, Tulunids, Ikhshids, Fatimids, and finally Ayoubids and Circassian and Bahrite Mamlukes abode their hour or two and perished, the pattern of history was repeated constantly. A strong and able ruler such as an Ibn Tulun or a Bars Bey would found a dynasty which flourished for a short time, to decay in the hands of inert and debauched successors. Thus, while Egypt remained rich, and by no means negligible in force of arms, the country to the

---

[1] Burckhardt, *Travels in Nubia* (1822), p. 474.
[2] Others had come earlier by way of the Red Sea. See Chapter IX, p. 97.

south of Assuan was never permanently administered, and the sultans were satisfied so long as it continued to yield revenue in tribute and port dues, and the supply of black troops for their armies and of gold and precious stones from the desert mines did not fail. In years of famine and want the Beja were apt to come raiding as they had done in Roman times, or to cut the trade routes from Aidhab to Kus, and on such occasions retaliation was necessary. Otherwise the sultans were content to let well alonè, and from 1187 onwards, after Saladin had crippled the power of the Latin kingdom of Jerusalem at Hattin, the pilgrim route to Aidhab became of very much less importance. Its end came in 1426 when the Mamluke sultan Bars Bey punished the plunder of a caravan carrying gifts to Mecca by an expedition which destroyed the port, and with it the power of the Hadareb in the Atbai.

Trade had already begun to go elsewhere, and only four years before the destruction of Aidhab the first Indian ship to berth there had entered the port of Suakin, which was to hold the monopoly of trade on the western shores of the Red Sea for four centuries to come. The fortunes of the Hadareb had been in decline ever since the middle of the fourteenth century, when the gold and emerald mines became exhausted and were abandoned in the reign of Mohammed Hassan ibn Kala'oun. The destruction of Aidhab completed a process already begun. Many of the Hadareb fled south, and there must have taken place something in the nature of a tribal resurgence resulting in the emergence of the tribes we know today. Legend agrees that the Besharin drove the Bellou (as they should now be called) from the Atbai late in the fifteenth century, though they remained still in the hills round Erkowit and Sinkat, retaining some of their serfs, and possibly acquiring others until about the middle of the sixteenth century, when the Fung first appeared upon the scene.

A Fung expeditionary force is alleged to have defeated the combined forces of the Bellou and the Arteiga in a battle fought at the gates of Suakin as early as 1506, and to have occupied the port. I consider this to have been quite impossible. Omara Dunkas, the first of the Fung kings, had established his kingdom in the Gezira with the help of the Abdullab only two years previously, and it is extremely improbable that his armies should have ranged so far so soon. The eastward expansion of the Fung, or rather of the Abdullab, occurred in the time of the great Mangilak, El Agib Abdullah, who defeated the Bellou in about 1580 or even earlier, and who is reputed to have spent much of his time at Suakin, and to have been responsible for the digging of the water tank now known as *Haffir el Fula.*

The Turks occupied Suakin in 1520 to find that the Arteiga had succeeded the Bellou as the masters of the port. The latter were steadily becoming less powerful, and about this time also the Hadendowa, according to tribal legend originally a warrior clan only forty strong, drove them south into the hill country beyond Khor Baraka. Legend also makes a certain Sheikh el Telu (Shaikatel) who has given his name to a mountain north-west of Sinkat, a king of the Bellou, and father-in-law of the Hadendowi hero who killed him and expelled his people. Their alleged pedigree opens as follows:

Mohd. Hadab (the Lion) (Sherifi)	= d. of Shaikatel, Chief of the ↓ Bellou
Mohd. Mubarak (Barakwin the Fearless) ↓	= Hadat b. Mohd. el 'Alawi (Sherifia)[1]
Hadendowa	

Tribal legend at the best is the least dependable of authorities and, imperfectly handed down by word of mouth with glosses and variations from generation to generation, results usually in a welter of misplaced dates and confused episodes. The chronology of the Beja tribes thus related is no less confused than any other, but making no more than an inspired guess it seems probable that the Besharin were the first to achieve any

---

[1] The name Hadendowa is thence supposed to derive from 'hadabendowa' = the lion people, or Hadatendowa = Hadat's people. Another explanation not inconsistent with the tribal view of itself is that it simply means 'hada endowa' = the best or first people.

separate tribal identity, and that they drove the Bellou from the Atbai in the late fifteenth century.[1] The Hadendowa appear next, and their expulsion of the Bellou from the Sinkat area can be dated at approximately the first quarter of the seventeenth century. The Amarar, who are first mentioned as living in the hills behind what is now Port Sudan, appear later still, and their emergence as a tribe did not take place possibly until nearly 1700, though mention is made of them fighting against the Hadendowa as early as the first half of the seventeenth century.

It was very probably about this time also that the northern Beja, under Arab influence, abandoned the spear as a weapon in favour of the broad-bladed Crusader sword with which they have since proved themselves such formidable fighters at close quarters. Among the southern Beja the spear remains still the most common weapon, partly because they were less subject to Arab influence, partly because the wearing of a sword became one of the privileges of the aristocratic castes who dominated them from the sixteenth century onwards. These spears are the exact type described by Makrizi, quoting Ibn Selim, and called by him *Saba'ia* on account of their length of seven spans, the blade being three and the haft four. Bent, on the other hand, holds that the name indicates an Axumite origin, but I myself am inclined to agree with Floyer that they are named from Jebal Saba'i in the eastern desert of Egypt at the source of the Wadi Zeidun, where there were iron mines. They were said to be obtainable only from a tribe of women who had the secret of their manufacture, had intercourse only with their clients, and killed all male children at birth.

The majority of the Beja were converted to Islam in the course of the fourteenth and fifteenth centuries, and accordingly

[1] The Besharin, whose memories seem to go further back than most, mention certain alleged ancestors, Anakw who lived in the eighth century and Kuka, a holy man who is alleged to have been a contemporary of the great Arab hero, Abu Zaid el Hilali, and who must therefore have flourished in the second half of the eleventh century. Another version perversely makes Anakw the nephew of Kuka by an unknown Arab father. It may be a truer one, as all Besharin are united in believing that Anakw was the true founder of the tribe.

found it politic to adopt a proper Arab ancestry. The Besharin and Amarar, as already mentioned, chose Kahil, sections of whose true descendants had long been resident among them; the Hadendowa, with greater independence, but no great originality, chose a Sherif. Such claims are of course absurd, yet the northern Beja as we know them today are not without their quota of Arab blood. There had in fact been so much intermarriage that the Beja strain was laced not illiberally with the blood of Kawahla, Guhayna, Hadarma, Rabi'a, Ashraf and other Arab interlopers who intermarried with them so that they have in them from Arabia not an inconsiderable amount both of the blood of Joktan and of Ishmael.

With the adoption of Islam they abandoned the matrilinear system and in doing so, 'their women', says Murray, 'had lost in freedom but gained in morality'.[1] I wonder. The Beja code is tolerably strict in theory, but it seems constantly to be broken, leading to brawls, killings, reprisals, and demands for compensation. The Amarar and Besharin are noticeably more lax than the Hadendowa, and in 1932 the Besharin tribal authorities were driven to disallow the usual compensatory fine of a she-camel, worth £E.8, for adultery on the grounds that husbands were deliberately encouraging the infidelity of their wives. De Bellefonds remarks on the beauty and easy virtue of Amarar and Balgab/Aliab women, among whom adultery was of very little matter, and goes on to say, 'l'on a commerce avec la femme de son frère et les parents au même degré'.[2]

All this, and a heavy incidence of venereal disease, which is having a marked effect on the birth-rate, point to a very considerable degree of promiscuity, and even among the stricter tribes complete licence is allowed during festivals and celebrations such as weddings and circumcisions, and a woman is still 'more valued by her husband if she gives proof of her attractiveness to other men, even by adultery'.[3]

[1] *The Sons of Ishmael* (1935), p. 22.
[2] *L'Etbaye* (1884), p. 188. (A custom still extant among the Shilluk.)
[3] Crossland, *Desert and Water Gardens of the Red Sea*, p. 26.

CHAPTER VIII

THE SUBJUGATION OF THE TIGRÉ
(750–1700)

La himmam min ata'al hewisto.[1]   TIGRÉ PROVERB

When, at some time in the eighth century, the last of the princes of Axum was deposed by the Shoans the history of the peoples whom they had once ruled lapses into obscurity and confusion, and almost nothing is known of them for some seven or eight centuries. The three southernmost Beja kingdoms mentioned by Yagoubi were probably states succeeding Axum, but they did not last long, and the country lapsed into anarchy and tribal war. Many of the tribes which then fought among themselves for domination or survival still exist, but know little of their past, and since they are now all Moslem are concerned mainly in establishing a spurious Mohammedan ancestry.

Of greatest interest are the Almada, of whom there are now some 4000 in the Sudan and about nine times that number in Eritrea. They appear, for a short time at least, to have established a kingdom on the coast between Massawa and Agig, and, even after their overthrow and enserfment by the Beit Asgadé in the early sixteenth century, seem to have retained something of their greater past, so that aristocratic castes had no scruples about taking their daughters in marriage. It is tempting to suppose that they might be none other than the Almodad, one of the lost tribes of the Joktan, of which, however, no evidence exists other than the suggestive similarity of their names, and they themselves declare that they are descendants of one Mahmoud el Madai, from whom also stem the tribes of Meikal and the Red and Black Targeila. The Hamasein and the Ad Fadil say they are the result of the union of a certain Mahmoud Abu Makrouh with a Bellou girl, the Abhasheila claim to be kin to

---

[1] 'The leopard grows fat with goats.'

80

the Beit Ma'ala on the distaff side, and the Rigbat have the misfortune to trace descent from Abdullah ibn Abu Bakr el Siddiq, whom everyone knows to have died childless. Such inventions are, of course, historically valueless, and all that can be said of these tribes is that probably they all derive from an ancient common stock, that their less distant forebears were vassal tribes of Axum which, when that kingdom disappeared, relapsed into a long period of tribal warfare, and of whom nothing is known until in the sixteenth and seventeenth centuries they were subdued and enserfed by small groups of better-armed invaders from the interior.

To this period belongs the rise and decline of the port of Badi' on the island of Eiré some fifteen miles south of the present village of Agig. It appears to have flourished between the years 600 and 1150 approximately, to have been suddenly abandoned, and to have been a ruin by the end of the twelfth century. Its inhabitants were of mixed Arab origin intermingled with some local (Beja) blood, who traded in local products such as tortoise-shell, pearls, ivory and alabaster. There remain of the port today only a number of underground cisterns, used by the herdsmen who graze their flocks on the island during the winter rains.

In the early sixteenth century the Beit Asgadé, founders of the Habab and other tribes of Eritrea, descended from the high plateaus of Akelé Guzzai and succeeded in overrunning the tribes of the coastal country between the Anseba and the sea, and in establishing themselves as their feudal overlords. In this they but aped the Bellou, at that time still the dominant authority in the area between Suakin and the district of Mazaga, at the confluence of the Atbara and the Setit, and also in the hinterland behind Massawa. This is very much the territory assigned to them by John Senex in his map dated 1709, and Sir Peter Wyche in *A Short Relation of the River Nile* published at the behest of the Royal Society in 1673, and 'procured from an inquisitive and observing Jesuit[1] at Lisbon, who had lived many years in

[1] This was Fra. Lobo, who visited Abyssinia in 1626.

Ethiopia' speaks of Suakin as an island occupied by the Turks but

of natural right belonging to a Powerful and warlike King whose Kingdom is called Bellow (anciently Negran), the Inhabitants are Moors, the Men, Horses, and Sheep the fairest I have ever seen; the water melons the most delicious I have ever tasted.[1]

This would appear to show that the Bellou still controlled the hinterland behind Suakin in the early part of the seventeenth century, though I do not think that there can be any doubt that they were in fact driven out by the Abdullab before 1600. The explanation lies in the fact that Fra. Lobo obtained most of his information from Abyssinian sources, and followed them in referring to all tribes of the Eastern Sudan generally as Bellou. The horses and the men who aroused his enthusiasm were possibly a detachment of the famous Fung cavalry.[2] The discomfiture of the Bellou at the hands of the Fung, or more probably of the Abdullab, took place approximately about 1580, when they were defeated decisively in a three-day battle at Asaramaderheib in the hills behind Agig. Their king, Mohammed Idris Adara, was killed, and they were driven, a broken remnant, to take refuge in the environs of Massawa, where they still remain.

The Abdullab army had contained a contingent of Sha'-adinab/Jaaliin who remained behind when the raiders withdrew, and like the Beit Asgadé before them, imposed themselves as a ruling caste upon the serf peoples whom the Bellou had abandoned, and whom they now designated (themselves included) as Beni Amer. According to tribal legend the name derives from Amer, whose father Ali Nabit, a wandering holy man of mixed Jaaliin and Melhitkinab descent, had met his

[1] *A Short Relation*, pp. 3–4. The Gwineb, the coastal plain north and south of Suakin, is still noted for its water melons.

[2] The Abyssinian chronicles refer frequently to raids on the Balaw all along the western frontier from Suakin to the Blue Nile, and it is clear from the context that they mean in fact either the Fung, or the tribes on the eastern boundaries of the Fung, referred to by the latter as the Sobaha.

death at the hands of the Bellou after having married a grand-daughter of Mohammed Idris Adara. Amer, when he grew to manhood, is supposed to have led the army which revenged his father's death, and the Jaaliin interlopers adopted the name of Nabtab (derived from Nabit) to distinguish themselves from their subject peoples. The caste system which they, the only true descendants of Amer, now adopted and imposed was much more rigorous than any which had preceded it, and while they adopted the language of their inferiors, intermarriage was forbidden, and caste distinctions between Nabtab and Tigré (as the serf peoples now came to be called) were most strictly enforced.

The pulverization and dispersion of the indigenous tribes was not yet, however, even now at an end. About the middle of the seventeenth century a group of Melhitkinab migrated from the Gash to the Red Sea as the result of a blood feud, and settled on the coast south of Agig, where they embarked on a long conflict with the Beit Bahalyai (an aristocratic caste of the Habab related to the Beit Asgadé) ending in the virtual extermination of the latter and the transfer of their serfs to the victors, and, in an even greater degree, to the Nabtab of the Beni Amer. The new tribal group thus created came to be known as the Aflanda, and its aristocracy as the Egeilab. It was about this time also that tribes such as the Haffara, Sinkatkinab, Labat, and Karabkinab, whether as a result of Bellou pressure or of that of other Beja tribes beyond them, removed into what is now the Agordat district of the western province of Eritrea, where they still remain. Thus by the end of the seventeenth century or thereabouts the whole coastal region between Khor Baraka and Massawa came to be occupied by three main tribal groups, the Habab, the Beni Amer, and the Aflanda, each consisting of a small, alien, superior caste imposing itself by force of arms on a very much larger number of indigenous serf peoples.

The decisive factor in these conquests (as also in medieval Europe) was the strong arm of the mail-clad horseman. The

Beja have always had a strong instinctive dislike of horses, animals which they have never been able to control or acclimatize, and they scorn all forms of protective armour other than their bullhide shields, relying for effectiveness in battle on speed, agility, surprise, and ferocity in attack. The warriors of the Beit Asgadé, Sha'adinab and Abdullab wore helmets and chain armour, and their horses were protected also by skirts of thick quilting. Against them the naked Beja spearman on foot stood little chance, and although the Hadendowa repulsed the Fung, the less warlike, meeker Tigré tribes succumbed easily, and fearful memories of the mailed and panoplied horsemen who could scatter them like sheep are still alive in them today.[1]

The ruling castes of the Beni Amer and the Aflanda being of Arab origin and Mohammedans, the conversion of their vassal tribes to Islam followed fairly rapidly, but among the Habab Christianity of a sort was to linger on into the nineteenth century. The Habab, who are now mainly an Eritrean tribe, need no longer concern us; it remains to examine more closely the tribal and social structure of the two remaining groups, and more especially that of the Beni Amer.

The caste system which the Nabtab enforced on their vassal tribes for some three centuries to come was borrowed in its entirety from their forerunners the Bellou who, as has been shown previously, brought the system with them from the Hadramaut—a system which in far earlier times had been imposed on the Hamitic tribes south of Khor Baraka by immigrants from Southern Arabia and the nobility of Axum.

The aristocratic caste of Nabtab had, however, the reputation of enforcing caste distinctions much more rigorously than

---

[1] There is a vivid description of the Fung cavalry in Bruce, who saw four hundred of them in camp near Sennar with the Vizier Adlan in 1772. Each man had a carefully kept mail shirt, a copper helmet without plume or decoration, a lance, a heavy broadsword and a small oval shield. Their equipment was completed by a heavy pair of poke gloves. He remarks also on the excellence of the horses 'all firmly made, and as strong as our coach horses, but exceedingly nimble in their motion'. (*Travels to Discover the Sources of the Nile*, vol. III (1805), p. 352.)

others, and so provide the classic example of the domination exercised by a small but extremely powerful ruling caste over a very much larger subject population. In the Sudan the Nabtab at no time numbered more than seven or eight hundred, their serfs not less than about eighteen thousand.

The relationship between master and serfs (the Tigré) was a purely personal one. All Tigré were born into serfdom as the serfs of individual members of the Nabtab nobility, a state of social inferiority from which there was no legitimate means of escape. Their condition, however, was not that of pure slavery: they had certain recognized rights, might own cattle and other property, and might not be sold or alienated by their masters, although transfer of serfs was practised in such transactions as marriages and blood settlements. If a serf was injured or killed by a Nabtabi the matter was one for adjustment with his master by payment of compensation, and should a serf kill a Nabtabi he was not himself punished, but his master was required to make restitution by transfer of the offender and five of his relatives to the dead man's family.

The system in theory, and at its best in practice, was, however, one of mutual obligation, and serfs paid tribute, and rendered certain aids and services, in return for protection, and in particular provision of a marriage portion and customary gifts on the occasion of births, circumcisions, and other ceremonies. One of its most striking features was the complete fragmentation of the serf class, and it is probable that in this the aristocracy carried out a deliberate policy of splitting up serf groups with the object of keeping them weak and divided, so that it was possible to find serfs of one small clan widely scattered among several Nabtab sections, and under control of different masters.

At the same time they enjoyed a considerable degree of physical freedom, and it was unusual for Nabtab and serfs to share the same encampments or grazing grounds. The lordly, indolent Nabtabi rarely went far afield, but the serfs, continually in search of water and grazing for cattle, ranged far and wide, and were often so far beyond effective reach that it might seem surprising that any connection was maintained at all. This was provided for in the appointment of a Nabtabi as *ba'ala'ad* or 'master of the camp' for the purpose of settling disputes, keeping the serfs in order, and entertaining guests. His tent was pitched in the centre of the camp, and he was entitled to a fee from the father of every girl married in the encampment.

Herding and milking of cattle were among the main services rendered by the Tigré, for by custom no Nabtabi might milk, and this remained until recently the principal distinction between those of aristocratic and serf origin. It was a distinction which applied to cattle only, the reason very possibly being that the Nabtab, coming of camel-owning stock, knew nothing about cattle, and left the herding and milking of them to the serfs to whom originally they belonged, so that in time the fact that the Nabtab never milked came to have the force of a caste distinction.

Among the Tigré themselves there is division into those who milk and those who do not, and as far as can be ascertained those who do are the Almada, Asfada, and some others, and those who do not are the Hamasein, Abhasheila, and Wilinnoho. As to how this division arose no one appears to be certain, but it is probable that they were not in origin serfs but only became so when they sought the protection of, or were defeated by, one of the dominant castes.

Serfs were allowed always to own cattle and other animals, and in this respect many of them became wealthier than their masters, but they were under obligation at all times to supply cattle for milking, butter, and other products on demand, and on occasions such as marriages and funerals had to produce animals for slaughter, milk or other produce in kind, as well as personal labour, and when their master moved camp they provided animals for his transport.

Latterly many of these obligations had fallen into disuse. Gifts of butter were offered rarely, and the custom of gifts on ceremonial occasions was more strictly observed by the serfs among themselves than between them and the Nabtab. The outward signs of serfdom had also become much less common, and it was often impossible at first sight to distinguish between some serfs and their masters. Dress, weapons, and the use of animals became more a matter of taste and convenience than of custom, and it was latterly no longer obligatory for a serf to refrain from riding a horse, wearing a turban or a sword, or from using a riding saddle on his camel. Intermarriage was, however, unknown, at least among the Sudan Nabtab, who have always taken exceptional pride in the elaboration of their marriage ceremonies and the higher dowries required for Nabtab girls.

Their most jealously guarded privilege, however, was the right to collect the tribute of their serfs, payment of which came to be regarded as a mark of serf status, and the right to collect it as an adjunct of nobility. At one time the laws of inheritance in serfs were no different from the usual *sharia* laws as to division of property, and all had a share, but early in the eighteenth century it became the practice for the eldest son to inherit all serfs, being at the same time under an obligation to see that they performed such necessary services as milking of cattle for other members of the family. Tribute at that time was a levy collected for the benefit of the tribal head (the *diglel*) and each Nabtabi collected it from his serfs with an extra levy for himself, known as the *rial mashangal*. The difficulties of collecting from a large number of widely scattered serfs led to a system of division whereby the head of the family allotted serfs for purposes of tax collection to various of his relations, each of whom was known as a *shirfaf*, a Tigré word meaning 'a fragment', and who were allowed to retain the *rial mashangal* for themselves. The family head was thus relieved of a great deal of trouble, and at the same time this arrangement satisfied the *amour propre* of a number of serfless relatives. When, with the advent of the Egyptian government, the levy for the *diglel* was replaced by a fixed tribute, and section chiefs were appointed about 1850, the system did not greatly alter save that the serfs had now to pay twice, once to the official chief, and again to the *shirfaf*. This system applied to all the Tigré-speaking peoples who, at one time or another, fell under the domination of the

Nabtab, and the Bellou when they fled south to Massawa, either abandoned, or were deserted by, the bulk of their serf followers.

Among those who were henceforward to be known as Beni Amer it is possible to distinguish two separate and very clearly defined groups. The first consisted of those remnants of the Tigré clans of whom the Almada, the Hamasein, and the Asfada are today the most important, and all of whom were peoples of ancient but mixed Hamito-Semitic stock. The second group was composed of a number of indigenous clans, the Labat, Sinkatkinab, Hafara, Libis, Hadoigoboiab, Karabkinab, and others, of much purer Hamitic stock than the Tigré group, and speaking To Bedawie, who appear to have been spread over the country between roughly Sinkat and the Atbara. They were then pushed south, whether by the Bellou in their retreat from the Atbai, or in company with them by stronger forces from the north is uncertain. The Hafara and the Karabkinab, being the most southern of the group, were driven into the Eritrean hills, while those to the north, if not enserfed by the Bellou, were at least for a time subject to them, and all eventually were absorbed into the Beni Amer. They remained in fact independent groups admitting a nominal serfdom only to the *diglel* as head of the tribe, and never at any time owed service to individual members of the Nabtab caste.

By some it is alleged that the latter group derives from the Hadendowa, and that it joined the Beni Amer only in fairly recent times, and it is probable that some such accretion, including the Hadoigoboiab and possibly some of the Labat, did in fact take place. Of the others it is more probable that they are of much older stock, the most ancient among the Beja which can now be traced.[1] In favour of the latter theory there are a number of supporting facts. Firstly, the language and strongly marked Hamitic characteristics of the whole group, secondly the name Sinkatkinab (the people of Sinkat) borne by one of its sections, although none are now to be found within hundreds of miles

[1] See Chapter III, p. 23.

of Sinkat,[1] and lastly the collective name by which they are now known is Hadareb, the same as that by which the Bellou had once been known.

They are today by far the most primitive, warlike, and untamable of the Beni Amer clans. Their capacity for suspicion and for viewing with concern is infinite: their avoidance of strange contacts is carried to most remarkable lengths. They remain as shy and unapproachable as the ibex of their native hills, and they have developed to a fine art the ability to live on practically nothing other than the milk of their numerous herds of goats. The fact that they never accepted more than a purely nominal serf status in Beni Amer society makes it unlikely that they were broken remnants of serf tribes left behind in the ebb of Bellou defeat. It is much more probable that they chose to accept association with the Beni Amer for purposes of protection, and that the name Hadareb was mistakenly applied to them on account of their language and previous association with the Bellou.

The contrast between the two so-called serf groups remains most marked to this day, yet in custom they are not dissimilar, and the difference lies in language, and even more noticeably in character and behaviour. The Tigré, from long years of fragmentation and servitude, have largely lost all pride of race, and have acquired a docility which makes them instantly amenable to authority, and at the same time shy, aloof and suspicious. Nevertheless, without virility or initiative, dumbly prepared to accept what others may decide for them, they are a malleable, rather sad and dependent people, incapable of concerted action. 'Les Tigré,' says Lejean, '. . .on les reconnaît aisément à leur teint plus foncé, à leur maigreur, à leur air un peu farouche, à leur miserables vêtements.'[2]

By contrast the Hadareb are in every way more nearly akin

---

[1] There are to be found in graveyards at Erkowit, near Sinkat, old graves of typical Beni Amer design, surrounded by the much more numerous Hadendowa burials of later date.

[2] *Voyage au Deux Nils* (1861), p. 142.

to the northern Beja tribes, whose language they speak; as shy and aloof as the Tigré, but for different reasons; impatient of interference, tough, independent and self-sufficient to a degree. Yet the kinship is there, not only between them and the Tigré, but with all other Hamitic groups, one of whose outward manifestations has been remarked in the Masai by Mrs Huxley as a 'strange blend of male arrogance and female plasticity'.[1]

The Beni Amer are not, therefore, a tribe at all in the correct sense of the word, consisting as they do of two widely distinct Beja groups, the one until recently dominated very closely, the other hardly at all, by a small, alien Arab aristocracy. When, therefore, some authorities talk about typical Beni Amer they are describing something which does not exist, for, depending upon from which group they made their selection, the subject-matter might be a typical Tigré of Hamito-Semitic origins, a Hadarbi, of a much purer Hamitic strain closely akin to the most ancient Beja peoples, or else a Nabtabi of predominantly Arab blood, but much diluted by intermarriage with other tribes of admitted aristocratic strain, such as Arteiga, Ashraf, and Ad Sheikh.

[1] Huxley, *The Sorcerer's Apprentice* (1951), p. 89.

CHAPTER IX

THE TURKIA EL SABIGA
(1520–1880)

All the vices of the oriental despot.
JUNKER (of the Governor of Suakin in 1875)

For the history of the three hundred years which elapsed between the Turkish occupation of Suakin and Massawa, and the conquest of the Sudan by Mohammed Ali the Great in 1821, we have to rely very largely on local sources which, as pointed out previously, are often scanty and confused.

Apart from an abortive attempt to occupy the highlands of Tigré in the second half of the sixteenth century the Turks were content with possession of a few strategic points along the coast, and left the barren hinterland and its inimical inhabitants well alone. Leo Africanus, by far the most knowledgeable writer on Africa of his time, after remarking that the Grand Signor had five viceroys in Africa, one of whom lived 'at Suachin for those places which are challenged by the Great Turk in the dominions of Prete Ianne', and who was backed by a fleet of twenty-five galleys based on Suez, goes on to say:

the King of Nubia maintaineth continuall warre... against certaine other people also dwelling upon the desert which lieth eastward of Nilus, and stretcheth towards the red sea not far from the borders of Suachin.... The people themselves are called Bugiha and are most base and miserable, and liue onely upon milk, camels-flesh and the flesh of such beasts as are taken in those deserts.[1]

The viceroy or bassa of Suakin, despite his resounding title and his galleys, had no control over the Beja, and Leo adds that they were, 'free from the Soldan's jurisdiction, for there his dominions are limited'.[2] The cartographers of the time incline to be more fanciful than accurate. Gastaldi's map of 1561 marks

[1] *History and Description of Africa*, vol. III, ed. Browne (1896), p. 837.
[2] *Ibid.* p. 904.

Zibid (Aidhab, destroyed in 1426) as well as Suakin, and Allagi in the Desert of the Buga. He also places a town called Fuingi in the kingdom of the Bellou, which according to him lay in the loop of the Nile by Abu Hamed. Janson's map of 1660 is scarcely more helpful. He had acquired considerable knowledge of Abyssinia from Portuguese sources, but is less accurate elsewhere. Like Gastaldi he continues to mark Zibid and to place the Bellou kingdom in Dongola, but Fuingi disappears and is replaced by Napata which has travelled east and lies in the desert far from the Nile. Leo's description is, however, supplemented by that of Don Juan de Castro, a hidalgo who sailed with Stefano de Gama's unsuccessful expedition against Suez in 1540. He writes of Suakin that it was:

one of the richest cities of the East, standing upon the coast of Abechi....It trades with both the Peninsulas of the Indies, particularly Kambaya, Tanasarin, Pegu, Malaka, within the Arabian Gulph to Juddah, Kairo and Alexandria; besides what it carries on with Ethiopia and the land of the Abeshins, from whence it hath vast quantities of Gold and Ivory,[1]

and goes on to say of the Beja that:

they are never at peace with their neighbours, but continually at war with everybody. They have no King or great Lord over them, but are divided into Tribes and Parties, over each of which there is a Sheykh. They build no Towns, nor other fixed habitations; their Custom being to wander from one place to another with their cattle.[2]

The sixteenth century, therefore, repeats in rather more authentic and credible form the accounts of earlier ages, and the nomad wandering Beja, carrying war into the Nile valley, raiding each others' herds, admitting, within the limits of their power, no central control, and fighting continuously over grazing and water, are as they always were, still are today, and no doubt always will be. This particular age, though largely

[1] Kennedy Cooke, 'The Red Sea Coast in 1540', *S.N.R.* vol. xvi (2) (1933), p. 153.
[2] *Ibid.* p. 159.

unchronicled, was for them one of unusual ferment, and tribal units as we know them today, the Amarar, the Besharin, and the Hadendowa, which were in process of emergence and consolidation, had to fight strenuously for survival not only among themselves, but also against the attempts of the Fung kingdom in the south-west to extend its influence into the Red Sea hills.

The extent to which the sultanate at Sennar made its power felt in the Eastern Sudan is by no means clear, and its attempts to extend the limits of its authority were only partially successful. Repeated expeditions were sent against the Beja, possibly in an attempt to discover and exploit the Red Sea gold mines. In this they were unsuccessful. They failed also to reduce the outpost tribe of Hadendowa, at that time a small, but exceedingly aggressive clan, who occupied the hill country round Sinkat and Erkowit, whence they had only shortly before expelled the Bellou, the Sinkatkinab, and others who are now classed as Beni Amer.

The Fung failed to penetrate to the Atbai, but as related in the previous chapter they had better fortune farther south against opponents less warlike than the northern tribes. There they succeeded, about 1600, in establishing a vassal administration (the Beni Amer) in the hills south of Khor Baraka, and it seems reasonably certain that they held the line of the Atbara with posts at Asubri and Goz Regeb, and from there dominated the Gash and Setit tribes, the Halenga, Hamran and others. Furthermore the Arab aristocracy who had imposed themselves by the sword over a large Beja serf population, and now called themselves the Beni Amer, relied, at least to begin with, on their support. Their chief (who came to be known as the *diglel*) was given a horned cap and the title of *mangil*; as late as 1730 the question of the succession was referred to Sennar for settlement, and the Abdullab chronicle states that the Abdullab were the overlords of 'ten districts of the Sobaha [i.e. the tribes of the Eastern Sudan] including the Nabtab, Halenko and Homran'.[1]

[1] Penn, 'Traditional stories of the Abdullab tribe', *S.N.R.* vol. XVII (1) (1934), p. 64.

Thereafter the sultanate was in decline and Beni Amer ties with Sennar were gradually relaxed.

Until early in the eighteenth century the northern Beja remained within the orbit of their hills and deserts north of the

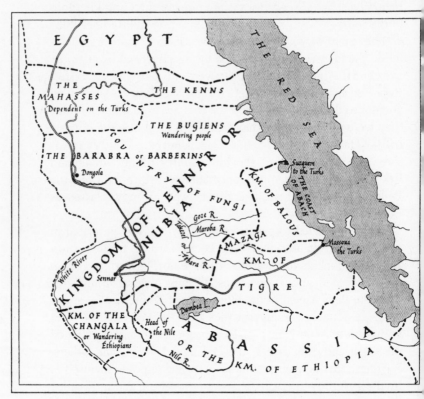

Map 4. Reproduction of part of the map of John Senex, 1709

nineteenth parallel. There then occurred one of those inexplicable spillings-over of a desert population in escape from conditions which have grown too hard for it, at the expense of the dweller in softer and less arid lands. In this the lead was given by the Amarar, whose original habitat was the hinterland immediately behind what is now Port Sudan; and being a politic as well as an ambitious tribe they tempered their expansion by intermarriage with such tribes as the Arteiga, Ashraf, Besharin and Hadendowa whom they found in their path. The catholicity of Amarar marriage relations is best illustrated by the following tree, compiled from details to be found in Sandars' article on 'The Amarar' in *Sudan Notes and Records*, vol. XVIII (2):

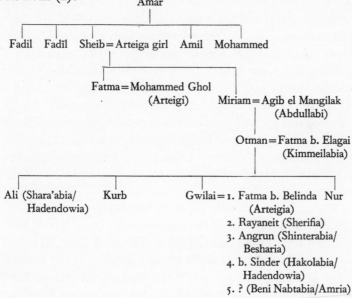

Whether the inclusion of Agib the Mangilak in the above pedigree can be accepted as historically accurate or not, it is nevertheless of chronological value, as he is known to have been killed at the battle of Kalkol in 1611, and it is thus possible to establish the existence of the Besharin and Hadendowa as fully developed tribes with clearly distinct sub-sections as early as the middle of the seventeenth century, or even earlier still. Sandars is of the opinion that the Mangilak had no place in Amarar history:

It is more reasonable to suppose that the story is merely an attempt to connect the tribe with the Fung aristocracy, and Agib's name is used either because he is a very well known *mangil*, or possibly because he had actually visited Suakin neighbourhood on the pilgrimage or for other reasons.[1]

The Abdullab historians certainly make no mention of the story, but there is very good reason to believe that Agib did visit Suakin and stay there for some considerable time. There is also nothing inherently improbable in a marriage or a liaison with a local girl and the Atamna or Othamna, a Red Sea tribe, are mentioned as the descendants of Agib in Abdullab pedigrees. In about 1725 under the leadership of Mohammed Agim (*c.* 1700–60) there began a definite infiltration of the Otman sections to the south and west which succeeded in driving a wedge into Besharin territory as far west as Musmar. This expansion, not by any means always peaceful, was consolidated under their most notable leader, Hamad Hassai (*d.* 1840),[2] and left them situated much as they are today, with the exception of the Nurab, who moved to Tokar only in the second half of the nineteenth century.

The next to move were the Besharin. It is related that about 1760 the Kammalab and Morghumab on the river Atbara, who as Aulad Kahil could claim affinities with the Besharin, invoked their aid against the Messellemia and Batahin in the Butana. Some Besharin sections may have reached the Atbara even before this, but a main migration now took place from the vicinity of Ariab under the great chieftain Hamad Omran which, from the point of view of their allies, ended by being almost too successful. The Besharin found conditions on the Atbara so much to their liking that they settled and have remained there ever since, its ample water supplies and better grazing being paradise to the nomads of the inhospitable Atbai. The genesis of the migration is adorned by the tale of how the Morghumab envoys found Hamad Omran with no more than the usual Beja complement of two or three tents. Disappointed, they never-

---

[1] Sandars, 'The Amarar', *S.N.R.* vol. xviii (2) (1935), p. 200.
[2] He is mentioned (Ahmed Assaye) by de Bellefonds as sheikh of the Amarar in 1833.

theless stated their business, expressed gratification at having
met so famous a warrior, and prepared to return. To convince
them Hamad summoned the tribe, and sent for two camel loads
of tobacco. When the warriors had assembled and each man
had filled his pipe there was no tobacco left.[1]

The last, but by no means least, of the northern Beja tribes
to seek easier living conditions in zones of heavier rainfall
were the Hadendowa. Their expansion southwards began
possibly early in the last quarter of the eighteenth century under
the famous Wailali Mohammed, a direct ancestor of the present
naẓir, the first to feel the weight of their arm being the Melhitkinab, a small but wealthy tribe which appears to have reached
the Sudan in two distinct groups and by different routes. The
main group crossed the Red Sea in the twelfth century and
settled on the coast and as far inland as Melhit (hence their
name) at the head-waters of Khor Windi and Khor Langeib.
The remainder came later by way of Dongola and the Atbara
and joined the main group about 1300. By the middle of the
eighteenth century, when they were so unfortunate as to find
themselves in the path of the Hadendowa, they were an extremely wealthy tribe, so rich in camels that their chief rejoiced
in the nickname of '*Gummad Hassal*' (the long camel halter).[2]
Their first clash with the Hadendowa resulted in their being
driven south into Odi, and from thence to Um Adam at the
northern extremity of the Gash Delta, where they found themselves pressed in on new antagonists, the Halenga.

Wailali Mohammed died about 1780 and lies buried in Khor
Langeib, but the pressure was kept up under his son Mohammed,
and was too strong to be resisted. The Halenga, Melhitkinab
and Sigolab were driven in on To Lus (Kassala) until, by the
beginning of the nineteenth century, the Hadendowa had

---

[1] Bruce's map of Ethiopia and the Eastern Sudan, drawn *c.* 1772, shows a
tribe of the Besharin, the Welled Omran, situated immediately north of the
Atbara and west of Goz Regeb.

[2] From whence the Gummud, the sheikhly section of the Melhitkinab,
takes its name today. They are mentioned by de Bellefonds (*L'Etbaye* (1884),
p. 129) as 'puissante tribu habitant le désert au Nord Est de Gooz Regeb'.

reached the Atbara and were firmly established in the Gash with their headquarters at Fillik, a bleak spot hardly enhanced by the usual Beja conglutination of matting tents round a convenient well-centre, which is described by Lejean, who saw it in 1860, as 'situé au milieu d'une plaine de la plus effrayante nudité'.[1]

Burckhardt, who travelled from Shendi to Suakin in the year before Waterloo, found the southern Besharin and the Hadendowa situated very much as they are today. He had a poor opinion of both. Of the Besharin he admits that they were 'a handsome and a bold race of people; they go constantly armed and are seldom free from quarrels' but adds that they were 'treacherous, cruel, avaricious and revengeful'.[2] The Hadendowa he condemns utterly: 'Towards strangers I never saw a more pitiless race of people.'[3] He later visited the Hadendowa market at Fillik in the Gash on his way to Suakin. He remarks on the fine quality of both cattle and camels, and has left a record of the wares displayed for sale which is interesting as showing how little the needs of the Beja have changed in the last 150 years. The list includes cattle, camel saddles, beads, tobacco, ropes, skins, salt, ostrich feathers, spices, mats and baskets, grain and local pottery, all of which are to be found in any similar market today.

The Hadendowa had by then reached the Atbara east of Goz Regeb, but the Besharin were farther east than they are now, and raided frequently into the Gash. The Hadendowa were too strong for them, however, and they were gradually forced farther west. How much farther the aggressive expansionism of the Hadendowa would have carried them, into the foothills of Eritrea, or into Shukria territory south of the Atbara, will never be known, because early in the third decade of the new century they found themselves up against new, and for the time being, more powerful antagonists, the armies which Mohammed Ali, the wali of Egypt, had launched southwards in 1821 to destroy the Fung kingdom and occupy the Sudan.

[1] *Voyage au Deux Nils* (1862), p. 43.
[2] *Travels in Nubia* (1822), p. 333.   [3] *Ibid.* p. 355.

The new rulers of the country had much to do, and apart from a devastating raid by Mohammed Bey the Defterdar, in 1823, following Ismail Pasha's murder at Shendi, the Egyptians for the first few years of their occupation paid very little attention to the eastern provinces, and the tribes of Taka and the Red Sea coast were left undisturbed. Mohammed Ali was, however, greatly interested in the mineral resources of the country, and in 1833 sent a French engineer, Linant de Bellefonds, to the Atbai to explore the old workings, and to him we owe a most interesting account of the country and of the northern Besharin. They were completely beyond the range of Egyptian administrative control, a fact which appears to have caused surprise when he reported it on his return to Cairo, and he had some difficulty in penetrating as far as Jebal Elba, which was inhabited by a number of robber clans, mainly of the Hamadorab (whom he calls the Ahmed Gourabieh) and the Shinterab. He reports nothing of the tribe as a whole which is not true of it today in almost every respect, and he is interested to note the physical resemblance of the Besharin to carvings to be found on ancient Egyptian monuments: 'je reconnus en eux le type de prisonniers représentés legendairement sur les bas-reliefs des temples et des tombeaux des anciens Egyptiens.' [1]

His summing-up of the Beja character in general has been quoted in an earlier chapter, but he remarks with particular astonishment on their ability equally to go with only minute quantities of nourishment for days on end, and to gorge themselves into a stupor whenever occasion offered, so that one man could devour a sheep at a sitting and remain torpid for several days, rather in the manner of a boa-constrictor, an ability which their descendants still retain.

He remarks also on their ability as breeders and riders of camels without mentioning either of the two breeds now most famous, the Ba Nagir and the Kiliewau, and records an ingenious custom of leaving she asses tied up in a remote spot when on heat so that they might be served by wild asses of the

[1] De Bellefonds, *op. cit.* p. 59.

desert, the foals of such unions being highly prized for stamina and pace.

Meanwhile the Sudan was not yielding the wealth expected of it, and in 1832 the governor-general, Ali Khurshid Pasha, decided upon a tax-gathering expedition against Taka. He acquired considerable quantities of cattle and even some gold, but retired after his forces had been severely handled by the Hadendowa in the forests of the Gash.[1] Eight years later Ahmed Pasha Abu 'Udan organized a large-scale expedition, his frankly avowed purpose being loot, and as much of it as he could get. He met with surprisingly little opposition, but his success in such matters as collection of tribute, or in the damming of the Gash was indifferent, and the only lasting result of his raid was the founding of Kassala as a military post to overawe the southern Beja. Mohammed Din, the all-powerful chief of the Hadendowa, whom Werne describes as 'of middle size, black-brown like all his race . . . his dress Arab, but his trousers of fine red cloth',[2] was captured by treachery, and died in imprisonment in Khartoum. His removal did nothing to pacify the tribe, and it was left to the next governor-general, Ahmed Pasha el Menekli, nicknamed the Butcher, to stamp out resistance by methods of the grossest and most revolting cruelty in 1844.

Scores of Beja were wantonly slaughtered and mutilated, wells were filled in, cattle maimed or driven away in herds. Men were killed for the Pasha's amusement, and one of his officers admitted that he practised swordmanship by trying to cut captives in half with one blow. Even the jealously guarded Beja women were handed to the Bashi-bazouks, and when the Pasha returned to Khartoum he took with him forty of the tribal notables to be hanged in the market-place. The resistance of the tribes was broken, and for forty years they never again attempted to dispute the occupation of their country.[3]

[1] De Bellefonds in the far Atbai heard rumours of this raid, and records that the pasha had been worsted by the Halenga and Hadendowa and retired to Khartoum in disorder (*op. cit.* p. 67).

[2] *African Wanderings* (1852), p. 155.

[3] Cumming, 'The History of Kassala and the Province of Taka', *S.N.R.* vol. xx (1) (1937), p. 19.

Nevertheless the Egyptians from now on were inclined to let them fairly well alone, and throughout this period, though the tax-gatherer and the bashi-bazouk went out to loot in the name of the state, it does not appear, the short period from 1873 to 1875 when Munziger was governor excepted, that there was much attempt at government in the Eastern Sudan. Those tribes on the coast who could avoid contacts with Suakin saw but little of their rulers, although there were posts at Tokar, Erkowit, and even farther inland at Temerein. The Atbara and the Atbai Besharin became from now on to all intents and purposes two separate tribes. The former paid tribute because, living on the river between Berber and Kassala, they could not avoid doing so; the latter probably paid none at all, despite an occasional tax-gathering raid from Berber, and they were never at any time under effective control.

The Amarar were assessed for tribute which ranged between £E.500 and £E.700. It was probably paid less often than not, and very little is heard of the Amarar until the Mahdia. Like the Hadendowa they engaged in transport work, and the Amarar *naẓir* from the vantage point of his headquarters at Ariab levied tolls on caravans passing up and down the Suakin-Berber road. Suakin still had a thriving trade in slaves, horses, grain, butter, a little gold, ostrich feathers and hides. Burckhardt estimated that two to three thousand head of slaves left the port every year, the export dues on horses being heavier than on human beings. Much surplus grain was exported from the Gash. Burckhardt says: 'no ship leaves Suakin for any part of the Arabian coast without having its hold filled with Dhourra from Taka'.[1]

Farther south, after the foundation of Kassala, posts were established in the friendly Beni Amer country, and in the newly acquired territory of Boghos, stretching from the Setit to Keren, and also at Goz Regeb and near Aroma in the Gash. That order of a sort was maintained can be gathered from the reports of numerous travellers who visited the country and

[1] *Travels in Nubia* (1822), p. 396.

survived to write their recollections of it, but they one and all comment on the unpopularity of Egyptian rule, and it is clear that the Beja tolerated it partly because it was not in fact very effective, and partly because of their fear of the superior weapons of the 'Turks'.

Taka was in fact a very poor province which had the distinction of always having the largest gap between revenue and expenditure, and by 1871 the state of affairs was such that tribute was £E. 40,000 in arrears and government staff, including the troops, were owed another £E. 36,000. Most of the expenditure was on the army, and when Munziger came to draw up his budget for 1874, out of a total of £E. 91,000 military expenses accounted for £E. 76,000. There was a serious mutiny of the troops at Kassala in 1865, owing to arrears of pay and the incompetence of their officers. The tribes were delighted to see their oppressors fighting, and took full advantage of the situation to escape payment of tribute and settle accounts among themselves.

The only tribe other than perhaps the Halenga (who soon regretted it) to welcome the coming of the Egyptians was the Beni Amer. They were a large unwieldy tribe who found themselves unhappily placed between more warlike peoples, the Abyssinians to the south, and the Hadendowa to the northwest. In this extremity they were prepared to welcome the Egyptians, with whom they duly came to terms in 1848, finding 'in the "Turks", the common enemy of all, a support against the Hadendoas'.[1] Nor were the aristocratic caste of the Nabtab at all averse to having the assistance of the authorities in dealing with their own very much more numerous, and occasionally restive, serf population. Collection of tribute was difficult, and here as everywhere else was paid only when troops were sent to collect it. The reigning *diglel*, Hamid Musa, exercised 'sur les diverses fractions de son peuple qu'une autorité nominale',[2] and was glad to lean on the *mudir* of Taka for support both

---

[1] Junker, *Travels in Africa* (1890), p. 95.
[2] Douin, *Le Regne de Khedive Ismail*, vol. III (1936), pt. I, p. 31.

PLATE IV

SUAKIN

against a turbulent nobility and the tribe's external foes. If tax-collection was difficult among the fairly amenable Beni Amer, elsewhere it was all but impossible, and of such sums as could be extracted only a portion ever reached the proper authority, chiefs, troops, officials, and not least the governor himself, all feeling themselves entitled to a prior share.

In 1863 Ismail Pasha, a grandson of Mohammed Ali the Great, succeeded his uncle Said Pasha as khedive of Egypt, and at once embarked upon a wildly ambitious and unpractical programme of expansion and development. In 1865 he took over Suakin once more from the Turks, and appointed as its governor an engineer officer, Ahmed Mumtaz, who 'soon displayed both his remarkable capacity for thinking out impracticable schemes for public works, and his malignity in the methods he used in trying to put them into practice'.[1] He was, however, the sort of man in whom the khedive delighted, and so in due course found himself promoted to be governor of the Eastern Sudan, and then of the south centre, including the Gezira. Initially he occupied himself with schemes of building a railway from Kosseir to Suakin, growing cotton at Tokar and Kassala (the produce of the latter area to be floated to Egypt by raft from Goz Regeb), improving the public buildings at Suakin, installing a new water system to be piped from the wells of Tamanieb, planting sugar-cane, roses, vines and even jasmine in the most unlikely places, and in making himself cordially detested by everyone, and by no one more than the governor-general, Jaafer Pasha Mazhar, who viewed his wild-cat schemes and lavish over-expenditure with disfavour, and vainly demanded his recall.

One of his least popular notions was that the unhappy tribesmen who were to be the beneficiaries of his brilliancies should provide labour for nothing, and this, combined with the long-established Egyptian custom of requiring stores, officials and their baggage to be transported free, resulted in a serious falling off in trade. Nevertheless, when Junker passed through Suakin

[1] Cumming, op. cit. S.N.R. XXII (2) (1940), p. 230.

in 1875, he remarked on its prosperity, and that duty on exports amounted to £.E. 60,000 annually. Some of the effects of Mumtaz's energy were witnessed by Captain Rokeby on the Atbara in 1871. 'The cultivation of cotton is arbitrarily imposed —the growth of corn almost prohibited.'[1] But not even Mumtaz could make the Beja grow cotton when they did not want to, and his efforts, except in Tokar where he used troops and convict labour, were everywhere a failure.

Werner Munziger, a Swiss, who succeeded Ahmed Mumtaz as governor of the Eastern Sudan, was of the same type, but had much less grandiloquent ideas, and reported to the khedive that though little cotton was now being grown in Tokar (1873) he was in favour of developing Agig as a port, rather than Suakin, with a railway to Kassala via Maman: 'Si donc Aghik est choisie comme centre politique de cette côté elle deviendrai sous peu la vraie capitale du commerce de tous les pays entre l'Atbara et la Mer Rouge.'[2] Ismail swallowed Munziger's ideas as easily as he had done those of Mumtaz. Troops were sent to Tokar, but liked it so little, and deserted with such frequency that Sudanese from Massawa had to be brought in to act as guards, and it was found easier to develop the cotton industry at Tokar by the use of convicts who, being chained, could less easily run away. From now onwards, however, the khedive had other things to interest him and the sole results of Mumtaz Pasha's and Munziger's economic schemes were the introduction of cotton to Tokar and the Gash, a ginning factory at Suakin, an incongruous factory chimney at Kassala, and a massive boiler and other machinery half buried in the sand between Tokar and Trinkitat.

From its first foundation in 1840 until about 1860 Kassala, which is described by visitors as a squalid and insanitary town, was merely a military post, but was now to become of increasing importance as the khedive's designs against Abyssinia took

[1] 'Narrative of an Expedition from Suakin to the Sudan', *J.R.G.S.* No. 44, p. 162.
[2] Douin, *op. cit.* pt. 2, p. 526.

shape. In 1872 Munziger occupied Keren and the district of Boghos with the connivance of a suitably rewarded governor, but when the advance was pressed farther the Egyptians were defeated at Gundet in 1875 (a battle in which the *diglel* of the Beni Amer lost his life) and suffered even worse disaster at Gura in attempting to retrieve the situation in the following year. Munziger was killed by the Danakil on the coast about the same time, and his death closed the chapter of Ismail's Ethiopian ambitions, and of Egyptian expansion in Africa.

CHAPTER X

THE MAHDIA AND THE RE-OCCUPATION
(1881–1900)

The sand of the desert is sodden red.—
Red with the blood of a square that broke.
The Gatling's jammed, and the Colonel dead,
And the regiment blind with dust and smoke.

SIR HENRY NEWBOLT

Mohammed Ahmed el Mahdi first proclaimed his divine mission in May 1881, and just over two years later scored his greatest success to date by the capture of El Obeid. During the whole of those two years there had been little sign of active unrest in the Eastern Sudan, and the Beja, remote and incurious as ever, and certainly not the Allah-inflamed fanatics they have sometimes been represented to be, might never have risen in revolt had there not appeared upon the scene a remarkable and domineering character to take advantage of a gross swindle perpetrated by the Egyptian authorities.

The Hadendowa, who were the principal carriers of government and trade goods between Berber, Kassala and Suakin, were given the contract for the transport of the reinforcements and stores forwarded to Hicks Pasha in 1883 by the Suakin-Berber route at the rate of seven dollars per camel. The government duly paid the full amount, but the troops and equipment safely delivered, the Hadendowa received six dollars less per camel than they had been promised. 'As for the Hadendowa revolt,' wrote Gordon to Sir Evelyn Baring in February 1884, 'it would appear to have been caused by the robbery of Rashid Pasha and Ibrahim Bey.'

To a tribe thus seething with indignation and resentment there appeared Osman Digna, with a message from the Mahdi preaching revolt against the Turk, and received a ready hearing. At a less opportune moment it is possible that this mission to raise the Eastern Sudan for the Mahdi might have failed. The

Beja are no zealots, though eager always for raiding and plunder, and he himself had few of the gifts of a popular leader. He was by way of being the black sheep of his family, Kurds who had emigrated from Diarbekir and had been long settled in Suakin where they had intermarried with local tribes, his own mother being of the Bushariab/Hadendowa. He had proved unsuccessful as merchant, slave dealer, and water contractor, and the early years of the Mahdia found him working in Berber largely because his long-suffering relatives in Suakin had had enough of him. In 1883 he visited the Mahdi shortly after the fall of El Obeid, and a month or so later returned to the Red Sea hills with the title of Emir and the Mahdi's mandate to raise the local tribes.

The man who for the next three lustrums was to be the best-known and most astute of the Mahdist emirs had at first sight but little to commend him. He was not popular with his own people, and he had none of the qualities which command respect among an independent and warlike race, for he seems to have had neither courage nor affability, nor generosity nor, even by their standards, a sense of honour. On the contrary, he was mean and churlish, and after his first experience of hand-to-hand fighting at Sinkat never again took an active part in battle, but developed an uncanny flair for judging the right moment at which to quit a stricken field. His reputation for harshness and treachery still lives, and he was, as reported by Wylde, 'of a morose and taciturn disposition'.[1] Yet for all that he had some unexplained gift of leadership, and was a great and unabashed liar, with great powers of persuasion; and in this, and a certain dour sagacity and formidable fixity of purpose, must lie the secret of his success in holding together an always formidable fighting force, for long the only one in the country to have to contend with opponents both better trained and better armed. He was himself under no illusions as to his lack of popularity: 'they follow me', he is once reported to have said, 'because I feed them... They are not people of the Faith

[1] '83–'87 in the Sudan, vol. I, p. 72.

but of the belly.'[1] He seems always, indeed, to have given more care than most Mahdist emirs to the problems of the commissariat. For the thirteen months from May 1889 to May 1890, when his strength was at a very low ebb, the receipts of the *Beit el Mal* at Afafit (Tokar) were: 132 slaves; 12,585 head of cattle, camels, etc.; 1000 tons (approx.) of grain; 85,617 dollars, and the bulk of this was expended in maintaining his forces.[2]

Such then was the man, small, ill-conditioned, unheroic and morose, who appeared in the Red Sea hills late in July 1883 preaching revolt against the government, and whose chances of success were fortuitously increased by the transport swindle, and by the utterly unexpected deference paid to him as emissary of the Mahdi by Sheikh Taha Maghzub, a local holy man, of great influence. Even so, he collected at first only a small following, some 1500 strong, with which he attacked the government post at Sinkat and was repulsed with loss by the garrison under Tewfik Bey, he himself being wounded and all but captured. Tewfik Bey, the one Egyptian commander to show initiative and ability, followed up the repulse by a successful attack on Osman's forces at Gabab, and had he been even moderately supported by his superiors, the probabilities are that the revolt would have been crushed.

Osman, twice defeated, was left with few followers, and his fortunes were restored only by the incompetence and futility of his opponents. The Egyptian authorities at Suakin made half-hearted attempts at conciliation which were brusquely rejected, and frittered away their resources of men and munitions in small, badly organized expeditions which were almost invariably overwhelmed. Tewfik received neither encouragement nor reinforcements, but a small force trying to make its way from Kassala to Suakin was cut to pieces in Khor Baraka by the Kimmeilab, and another, sent to the relief of Tokar in November 1883, was defeated by a few ill-armed Beja only a day before Hicks met even worse disaster in Kordofan. A regiment of

[1] Jackson, *Osman Digna* (1926), p. 176.
[2] Sudan Government Archives.

Sudanese was then brought from Massawa, thrust into battle insufficiently supported and without proper water supplies, and perished almost to a man. After that the Egyptians could only cower behind the defences of Suakin while Osman gained new

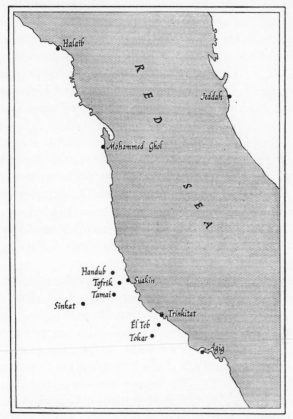

Map 5. The Red Sea battle area, 1883–91

courage and adherents, more particularly from the Hadendowa, whose disaffection effectively closed the Suakin-Berber road, and thus contributed materially to the fate of Gordon in Khartoum, and of the remaining Egyptian garrisons in the Sudan.

General Gordon arrived in Khartoum in February 1884 with somewhat ambiguous instructions to disengage and withdraw the Egyptian garrisons, and about the same time the Egyptian government, alarmed by the defeat at El Teb, sent a force of gendarmerie to reinforce Suakin (the British government refusing to sanction use of regular troops on the ground that they were as yet insufficiently trained) with orders to remain, except under the most favourable circumstances, on the defensive. Tokar and Sinkat were both closely invested, and the gallant Tewfik and the garrison of the latter post were nearing the end of their resources. In an ill-conceived attempt to relieve pressure on Sinkat, which he knew himself to be incapable of relieving directly, General Baker, who commanded the gendarmerie, moved on Tokar via Trinkitat, and on the previous battlefield of El Teb his force of 3500 men was utterly routed by about 1200 Beja with the loss of all his guns, 2500 in killed and missing, and 3000 rifles which his panic-stricken troops threw away in the course of their flight. The Beja were armed only with sword, shield and spear, and some not even with that, as it is recorded that they used their heavy camel sticks with devastating effect against the legs of the horses of the Egyptian cavalry.

A few days later Sinkat fell. Tewfik Bey marched out with the remnant of his starving garrison and met a soldier's death a few miles on the seaward side of the post he had so ably defended. He was, as Osman Digna (who was not given to praising his enemies) wrote in a letter to the Mahdi, 'one of the ablest of the accursed Ala el Din's men, and renowned for his bravery'.[1]

The fall of Sinkat and Baker's disaster at El Teb aroused much popular indignation in England, and a nervous Liberal Cabinet, which had already disclaimed responsibility for the Sudan, and had been very lukewarm about what it described as Gordon's essentially pacific mission to Khartoum, now allowed itself to be swayed by popular clamour into taking military action in the Eastern Sudan, and despatch an expedition

[1] Osman Digna to the Mahdi. August 1885. Wingate, *Report on the Dervish Rule in the Eastern Sudan* (1891).

which, since it had no clear object, resulted in senseless and unnecessary slaughter. The government once spurred, acted with commendable promptitude, and by March General Graham was at Suakin and able to take the field with 4000 British troops.

Seeking to relieve Tokar, Graham learnt on arrival at Trinkitat, that the garrison had already surrendered. Both Gordon and Baring advised against further action, but the Cabinet, fearing the reactions of an indignant electorate, allowed Graham to advance, so that the barren dunes of El Teb once again echoed to the sound of rifle fire, but this time with very different results, and 1500 Beja dead testified to the efficacy of modern weapons in the hands of disciplined troops. They had revealed once again, however, that they had not lost the art of dealing with cavalry. 'The real opposition', wrote Royle in a description of a charge by the British cavalry under General Stewart, 'came from the spearmen, who rising at the precise moment attempted to hamstring the horses...or else drive home their heavy spears.... The Sudanese also threw boomerang-like clubs of mimosa wood at the horses' legs, thus bringing many of the animals to their knees.'[1]

There being nothing else to do Graham withdrew to Suakin, to sally out again in an attempt to clear the country and at Tamai (eight miles south-west of Suakin), advancing without proper precautions through thick scrub, paid the penalty of having one of his squares broken by the rush of Beja swordsmen, a feat which was to give inspiration to more than one British poet,[2] and an ugly situation was restored only after some bitter fighting.

Graham's force was recalled in May 1884, the Cabinet having recovered from its temporary panic, and being once more pacifically inclined. The last word remained with Osman Digna.

[1] *The Egyptian Campaign—1882–85* (rev. ed.), 1902, p. 285.
[2] Kipling's verses on the 'Fuzzy Wuzzy', some of which are quoted on p. 113, are the best known. Newbolt's lines, quoted as a chapter heading, come from 'Vitae Lampada', to be found in *Poems Old and New* (1915), p. 78.

'The English', he reported in a letter to the Mahdi, 'did not stay long, for God had struck fear in their hearts.'[1] The expedition had, in fact, been wholly inconsistent with the declared policy of evacuation. It achieved nothing. Osman Digna was not crushed, Gordon's peaceful overtures in Khartoum were hampered by the bloodshed on the Red Sea coast, and the only useful purpose to which Graham's victories might have been put, that of a dash to Berber to re-open the Suakin-Berber road, was rejected almost as soon as suggested. For no other reason, therefore, than to stave off a vote of censure in the House of Commons the government had been wholly false to its own policy, and seven hundred British casualties, and nearly 5000 Beja dead, was apparently but a small price to pay for the continuance in office of Mr Gladstone and his colleagues. The soldiers who fought in so inglorious a cause found more to admire in their enemies than in either of the governments, Egyptian and British, for whom they were sent to fight:

The story of the three English expeditions that have been despatched to the Sudan [wrote de Cosson in 1886] has a painful sameness. They have all been sent out too late, and in order to allay popular sentiment when the Government was threatened with censure. We were in fact an...army making a political demonstration to keep a...Government in power.[2]

Worse was yet to come. The government which had been so prompt to avenge Baker and Tewfik by force of arms was less concerned about the fate of its envoy in Khartoum. Mr Gladstone in the House of Commons, unable to 'accept simple evidence of a plain fact which was patent to much less powerful intellects than his own',[3] split hairs regarding the difference between being surrounded and hemmed in, and the relief expedition came too late to save Gordon from death on the palace steps at Khartoum in January 1885. An indignant country demanded immediate action, and the government could think

[1] Sudan Government Archives.
[2] *Days and Nights of Service* (1886), p. 20.
[3] Cromer, *Modern Egypt*, vol. II (1908), p. 17.

of nothing better than a repetition of the Red Sea expedition of 1884. General Graham was once again sent to Suakin, and a contract was made with the firm of Lucas and Aird for the construction of a railway from Suakin to Berber. The railway advanced, under much difficulty, as far as Otao, eighteen miles inland, and was abandoned in May after two months' work costing some £850,000. The British troops, after fighting two hard-fought engagements at Hashin and Tofrik (better known as McNeill's Zeriba) were withdrawn at the same time. In this last battle a convoy of British and Indian troops was taken by surprise while constructing a thorn fence for the protection of their camp, and in a desperate mêlée lasting only twenty minutes eventually drove off the enemy with a loss of 1500 dead as against their own casualties of less than 300.

In all these engagements the Beja fought with the utmost courage and ferocity, and even when severely wounded were a source of danger to any who approached them. Women and children fought alongside the warriors. At Graham's Teb, 'lads of twelve, fighting desperately, fell dead in the shelter trenches, with their teeth set and their hands grasping their spears',[1] and at McNeill's Zeriba a boy of about the same age was seen throwing stones at the British line amidst a hail of fire. In all the writings of the time, animadverting on the Suakin campaigns, and on the ineptitude of the government, there appears almost without exception a warm admiration for the enemy against whom we fought. The desperadoes who crept nightly between the lines to knife the sentries, and who charged unflinchingly into a hail of death on half a dozen battlefields, had qualities which appealed to the British soldier and earned his respect:

> 'E's a daisy, 'e's a ducky, 'e's a lamb!
> 'E's an injia-rubber idiot on the spree,
> 'E's the o'ny thing that doesn't give a damn
> For a Regiment o' British Infantree![2]

[1] Royle, *op. cit.* p. 284.
[2] Kipling, *Verse*, Inclusive ed. (1925), p. 393.

Men and money had once again been squandered to no purpose, and it was the opinion of one observer that 'the case against Mr Gladstone's administration is so black that historians will be more likely to exercise their talents in finding excuses and explanations than in urging the indictment'.[1]

In spite of nearly 10,000 killed in battle Osman Digna was still unvanquished, and continued intermittently to make a nuisance of himself on the outskirts of Suakin. Kassala fell in July 1885 after a prolonged and gallant defence, Ras Alula, who had failed to relieve it as he had promised, scoring a belated revenge in the decisive defeat of a Dervish raiding force at Kufit.

The casualties which they had suffered in the battles on the coast had nevertheless had a cooling effect on the ardour of the local tribes, and Osman Digna began to find difficulties in maintaining an adequate fighting force in the field. His main strength was drawn from the Hadendowa, some of the Atbara Besharin, several sections of the Otman/Amarar, and some of the Tokar tribes such as the Hassanab, Ashraf and Kimmeilab. From now on, however, all but a few of the most devoted were to desert him, and he was forced to rely more and more on re-inforcements of Baggara and riverain tribes, who were very far from popular, and as the Beja began to fail him Osman's full ferocity was unleashed.

The Amarar were the first to suffer his displeasure. This tribe, by reason of its geographical situation, found itself throughout the Mahdia between two fires, and attempted to be on both sides at once, with that lack of success which is apt to attend on those who are unaccustomed to delicate balancing tricks. Their waverings aroused the harsh temper of Osman, and in 1886 he executed the Amarar *nazir*, Sheikh Hamid Mahmoud, together with the sheikh of the Nurab section. If his object was to intimidate the tribe he failed to do so, and the only result of the murders was to alienate it completely, and during 1881 Amarar

---

[1] Churchill, *The River War*, vol. 1 (1901), p. 107. It is only fair to add that Gladstone was returned to power by a large majority in the elections of 1885.

friendlies brought off several successful raids, including the capture of Tamai, with seventeen guns.

At the same time Osman lost the support of the Gemilab/ Hadendowa, a powerful fighting section, and of the Ashraf, and from now on his fortunes were on the decline. Those tribes which were not openly hostile were in a state of uncertainty and disinclined for further warfare. By 1887 his forces had dwindled to such an extent, and he himself had become so thoroughly unpopular, that the Khalifa sent the Dongalawi emir Abu Girga to reinforce him with a considerable force of Baggara. This made matters not better but rather worse. The two emirs spent much of their time in quarrelling, the Beja were quick to resent the intrusion of alien tribes, and many took refuge in the hills. The Baggara and the Hadendowa came to blows almost at once, and for a time a state almost approaching civil war existed, with the latter getting very much the better of it. Nevertheless, Osman still held his ground in front of Suakin, and in 1888 enjoyed a slight revival of fortune. Colonel Kitchener failed in an attempt to capture him at Handub, and the seige of Suakin from then on was pressed more closely.

That this was possible, despite local disaffection, was due to a number of causes. The awe in which his name was held, both within and without the town, still counted for much; the Amarar and Hadendowa insurgents, though they swore repeatedly to combine against him, and even made some attempt to do so, invariably frustrated achievement by quarrels among themselves. He had, moreover, considerable forces of Baggara at his disposal, and as long as he held Tokar, the granary of the coastal areas, he was able to feed them and maintain them in the field. The authorities in Suakin had also permitted free trade in grain so as to encourage local desertions. This it may have done, but much inevitably found its way to the Dervishes and increased their resources. Osman was also able to use some of the anchorages north of Port Sudan for the import of supplies from the Hedjaz, and a profitable trade developed which only ceased when a government post was established at Mohammed Ghol.

To relieve Suakin the sirdar (General Grenfell) brought down Egyptian troops and defeated the investing force at Gemmeiza, just outside the walls, in December 1888. Even so, the redoubtable emir was not yet quelled; he had always maintained posts in the desert at Ariab and Abu Duiem, and in April 1889 scored a minor success with a raid on the Besharin port of Halaib near the Egyptian frontier. The raiding party was wiped out shortly afterwards at Meisa, and the Atbai Besharin remained almost unaffected by the Mahdia, unlike those on the Atbara, who were heavily involved. Cameron, who was British Consul at Suakin, thought that the Mahdia would have the effect of changing the tribal balance of power. 'Whole mountain districts have been depopulated. The authority of the great sheikhs has been upset, and the future is in the hands of a few less powerful sheikhs and tribes who have kept aloof from the fighting, and who are, in consequence, relatively much stronger than before.'[1] In fact the Mahdia had less lasting effect than might have been supposed. The tribal balance of the Amarar and the Besharin was for a time upset it is true, but the Hadendowa, despite heavy losses, were soon as powerful as ever they were before.

But the sands of Dervish dominion were running out. In 1891 Osman fought his last battle on the coast in defence of Tokar, and was defeated with the loss of 700 killed, it being noteworthy that of the seventeen minor emirs who fell in the battle only one was of local origin. From now on he led a precarious existence, raiding for grain and cattle from a base at Adarama on the Atbara. In 1894 the Italians seized Kassala and, after repulsing several attempts at recapture, handed it over to an Anglo-Egyptian force in 1897, their defeat at Adowa in the previous year having cured them of colonial ambitions for the time being. Meanwhile Dongola had been re-occupied in 1896, and in 1898 the main advance began. Osman, with a few Hadendowa and Besharin, was present at the battle of Atbara which ended in the defeat and capture of the Emir

[1] 'On the Tribes of the Eastern Sudan', *J.R.A.S.* No. 16 (1887), p. 290.

Mahmoud, but escaped with his following almost before the battle had begun.

In September 1898 the battle of Omdurman settled the fate of the Sudan; it was less, indeed, a battle than a massacre, in which reckless courage was helpless against the destructive power of modern weapons. The issue was settled at bullet range, and only in one corner of the battlefield did the two forces come to close quarters, where the 21st Lancers fell into a trap such as had nearly brought disaster to Graham at Tamai fourteen years before. The majority of the Dervishes who lay in ambush in Khor Shambat were Beja of Osman Digna's command, and for the last time in history the swordsmen from the Red Sea hills faced a charge of cavalry. Of how they acquitted themselves let one who took part in it give evidence:

Riderless horses galloped across the plain. Men, clinging to their saddles, lurched helplessly about, covered with blood from perhaps a dozen wounds. Horses, streaming from tremendous gashes, limped and staggered with their riders. In 120 seconds five officers, 65 men and 119 horses out of less than 400 had been killed or wounded.[1]

In the Eastern Sudan administration by this time had long reverted to normal, and from 1891 onwards peacetime conditions prevailed. Suakin was opened to trade, the Berber route once again became practicable, and cotton was cultivated over an ever-increasing area of the Tokar Delta. The Beja had suffered heavily both as the allies and opponents of Dervish rule. The Hadendowa, the tribe most heavily involved on the Dervish side, had been thinned by famine, disease and war, yet even so had managed to consolidate its hold on the Gash and the middle Atbara. The Amarar were in a state of disintegration, and only the Fadlab sections preserved any sense of tribal unity. The rift between the Atbai and Atbara Besharin was widened. The Beni Amer, protected to some extent by Abyssinian and Italian

[1] Churchill, *The River War*, vol. II (1901), p. 138.

victories, yet suffered heavy losses and serious tribal derange-
ment, and lesser tribes like the Melhitkinab and Hamran were
all but exterminated. Thousands had been killed in war, in
battle against the British, or by the Dervishes who harried un-
mercifully all those who showed the slightest half-heartedness
in their cause, and even more had perished from want and
hunger in the terrible famines of which that of the year 1887
was the worst. Few of the great tribal leaders survived, it
being the Khalifa's policy that they should not: and throughout the Beja country there was everywhere war weariness and
disillusionment.

The new *Turkia* was therefore accepted with better grace
than might have been expected, and there remained only the
troublesome personality of Osman Digna who, escaping with
characteristic forethought from the battlefields of Omdurman
and Um Debeikerat, was everywhere regarded with more appre-
hension than he really deserved. The days when he had power
to rally the Beja were over, yet it was to their territory that he
fled after the final defeat and death of the Khalifa at Um Debei-
krat in 1899. The Gemilab/Hadendowa gave him sanctuary
in the wilds of the Warriba hills, but they had long ceased to
have cause to love him, and as soon as possible arranged for his
capture by the authorities. He was deported to Egypt, but
ended his days, the last of the Mahdi's emirs, in honourable
confinement at Halfa in 1926. A remarkable and enigmatic
character, his memory is now all but forgotten among the
tribes whom he had once led and bullied, and the announcement
of his death at a tribal meeting in 1926 caused, as District
Commissioner, Hadendowa, reported at the time, 'about as
much sensation as the decease of the Kaiser might have evoked
in a remote Highland village'.

The eastern boundaries of the Sudan as demarcated by agreement after the re-occupation were not those of Turco-Egyptian
times. The province of Boghos which had been occupied by the
Khedive Ismael had been returned to Ethiopia as the price of
assistance in evacuating the Egyptian frontier garrisons, but

was now held by Italy as part of her colony of Eritrea which, despite her defeat at Adowa in 1896, she had managed to establish in the triangle of coastal country north of the Setit. The new boundary left the bulk of the southern Beja in Eritrea, including about two-thirds of the Beni Amer. The remaining third in the Sudan was further subdivided, one group living near Kassala and the other in the Red Sea hills south of Khor Baraka.

CHAPTER XI

RECENT HISTORY
(1900–1950)

La liberté est si chère à ces hommes du desert qu'ils préfèrent
encore leur état à l'existence plus aisée.   DE BELLEFONDS

This chapter on recent developments among the Beja is written
in the belief that their reactions to modern methods of administration are not without interest. The picture which it will
present is necessarily incomplete, and half a century, or rather
the much shorter period which has elapsed since the administration of the Beja first received serious attention, is all too
short a time in which to draw many definite conclusions. Nevertheless this period of stable government, in which law and
order have been impressed with a firm hand, and in which their
particular problems have been the subject of sympathetic study
by the authorities, have not been without their effect. Materially
they have benefited considerably, by improvement of water
supplies and provisions of schools and dispensaries: and
standards of living have been raised, however slightly and un-
evenly, by encouragement of the *dom* nut trade and participation in the cotton-growing schemes in Tokar and the Gash
Delta. Intertribal warfare has been reduced to a minimum;
famine and plague, though never far distant, are no longer the
dread scourges of the past, and when they do occur the Beja can
expect immediate succour in the form of medical aid and food
supplies to tide them over the worst periods.

The government demands in turn a certain regard for its
conception of law and order, and some measure of co-operation
and promptitude in the payment of taxes: and it is in these two
spheres that the measure of administrative success or failure
can best be judged. Law and order are in the main observed,
and there is growing appreciation that murder, blood-feuds
and intertribal raiding are social crimes which no properly

constituted government will tolerate, yet sword-fights and killings are all too common, and it was possible as recently as 1951 for an armed policeman who attempted to intercept six Hadendowa raiding Beni Amer cattle to be cut down with over sixty sword wounds on his body. As for tribute collection, while the money does eventually come in, and there are few arrears, it does so only at the cost of a good deal of sweat and toil for all concerned.

In the field of education the government has expended a great deal of effort for no great return, and while the Beja are prepared to admit the benefits of modern medicine, they do so with scepticism and the conviction that a Koranic text or a red-hot iron is infinitely more efficacious, and only padlock and chain will keep many of them in hospital for a simple operation which would relieve them once and for all of a painful and wasting disease.[1] Even where his animals are concerned he has been slow to realize the value of prophylactic and curative drugs. He prefers other methods. The following is an eye-witness account of a camel undergoing veterinary treatment at the hands of its master:

Its tongue had been pulled out, and was being vigorously washed and scraped. Finally the camel owner took his knife and made numerous incisions in the under part of its tongue which he rubbed until the blood flowed freely. The operation was concluded by forcing a handful of donkey dung down its throat.[2]

As a cultivator he has many failings, and though years of patient endeavour by the authorities, and the high prices to be derived from cotton in boom years, have weaned him a little from his inherent dislike of organized agriculture, his interest therein is not that of the husbandman carefully tending the soil which is his livelihood, but of the opportunist availing himself of the quick profits of a cash crop with which to buy more

[1] The one exception perhaps is D.D.T., the efficacy of which as an exterminator of lice was very quickly recognized and appreciated.

[2] Clark, 'The Manners, Customs and Beliefs of the Northern Beja', *S.N.R.* vol. XXI (1) (1938), p. 22.

animals and indulge himself in various ways, so that profits disappear rather more easily than they were won.

If there were at any time any hopes therefore that the Beja might be induced to change his skin, there are at the time of writing very few signs of his willingness to oblige. Nor, living as he does, and in surroundings such as his, is it desirable that he should do so to any great extent. He has lived as a coney of the rocks and as the wild ass of the desert for hundreds of years, and since it seems likely to be his fate to go on doing so for hundreds of years more, the less his conventional and highly successful way of life is upset the better, and he is best served by those who insist only on the essentials of good administration, and who, while seeking by all means possible to improve and ameliorate his barren existence, are content otherwise to let him well alone to do things in his own way.

For the first twenty years of the condominium government little was heard of the Beja, and that little none of it good. It may be that there was little to tell, and it is indeed best to admit that as they were scarcely administered, so they were all but unknown and uncared for. The new government, busy with the pacification of an enormous area, and with the evolution of a system of administration for a great variety of peoples, naturally gave first attention to areas better known and more productive, and to peoples more accessible and amenable than the Red Sea hills and their shy, truculent and unapproachable inhabitants. Little could be hoped for from a people whose language none could speak, who avoided contact with authority as others did the plague, and about whose history, customs, and characteristics almost nothing was known.

So it was that the Beja continued happily enough in their wild and untrammelled ways, rendering obedience and paying tribute where they could not escape it, indulging as ever in local squabbles and sudden tribal forays, and reducing those responsible for their administration to despair and all forms of uncharitableness. The coastal areas were naturally those most closely administered, from the headquarters of Red Sea Province at Suakin, and posts were established at Tokar, Agig, Mohammed Ghol, and Halaib. The Atbai Besharin were supposedly administered from the latter post, but were switched back and forth in bewildering fashion between Red Sea and Berber Provinces, and were not finally handed over to Red Sea Province until 1923.

Cotton was first cultivated at Tokar after the re-occupation in 1891 when about 2000 acres were sown, but the area did not come under serious development until about 1905–6, since when an average of about 50,000 acres have been sown annually. The Baraka flood which waters the Delta is erratic, so that in recent years as much as 120,000 and as little as 15,000 acres have been available for cultivation. Stability under such conditions is not to be looked for, nor are the Beja a thrifty people who take thought for the future, so that their fortunes in Tokar are apt to fluctuate rapidly between affluence and poverty.[1]

The innate difficulties of administering such a people were very greatly enhanced by the fact that they were subject to no single administrative authority, but found themselves split tribally and even sub-tribally by a number of arbitrarily drawn administrative boundaries. Thus the Amarar belonged mainly to Red Sea Province, but some sections, with the Atbara and Atbai Besharin, found themselves at times under Berber Province, and the Hadendowa and Beni Amer were divided between Red Sea and Kassala Provinces. Tax evasion became thus a matter of such ease, and gave such opportunity for the bedevilment of the authorities that the Beja can almost be excused for finding it irresistible, and when methods of assessment and collection differed from province to province, as they did between Red Sea and Kassala Provinces, primeval chaos became confusion yet worse confounded, and one who was to be connected with them intimately in a subsequent complete and successful realignment of policy wrote of them at this time:

[1] In 1904–5, 7425 acres at Tokar yielded 29,039 kantars of cotton valued at £E. 25,873, in 1950–51 (a bumper year) 60,000 acres yielded 352,445 kantars valued at £E. 2,617,000.

'Tribal unity and intertribal amity naturally suffered. For many years public security was precarious, co-operation with the government negligible, and tax collection a nightmare.'[1]

This highly unsatisfactory state of affairs continued for many years, the only achievement of merit being the appointment in 1916 of Ahmed Mahmoud, a son of the *nazir* executed by Osman Digna, as *nazir* of the united Amarar, though for long the Fadlab sections refused to follow an Otman chief. Particular attention was, however, directed to the shortcomings of Beja administration in 1918, when a small band of Hadendowa led by a West African fanatic successfully rushed the fort at Kassala with the direst consequences to its garrison of Egyptian troops, and though easily suppressed it was shrewdly suspected that the outbreak resulted from a very general disaffection. In the inquiry which followed, the administration of the Beja, and of the Hadendowa in particular, was severely criticized: '... largely hostile, living in very inaccessible country, and not only imperfectly administered, but largely unknown.'[2]

Little was done to improve matters, largely because with shortage of staff and of means little could be done, and the tug of war between the Red Sea Province and other provinces over Beja administration continued. In 1926 a district commissioner, newly transferred from Kordofan, commented on 'the ramshackle nature of the tribal structure, and lack of tribal discipline', and condemned the whole administration for its divisions and fragmentations which were inimical to orderly government, and made tax collection all but an impossibility. There was less justice in the first part of this criticism than in the second. Even today it would be an exaggeration to describe any of the Beja administrations as tribally compact, and to the casual observer it is sometimes surprising that anything gets done at all. Twenty years ago appearances were no doubt closer to facts than they are now, but no administration of the Beja in

[1] Newbold, 'The Beja Tribes of the Red Sea Hills', in *The Anglo-Egyptian Sudan from Within* (ed. Hamilton, 1936), p. 160.
[2] Sudan Government Archives.

which efficiency and discipline are not tempered with the utmost latitude in performance, and which reposes no confidence in the ability of the apparently haphazard tribal machine to produce approximately the result required could be other than unworkable.

As regards fragmentation, the critic of 1926 was on surer ground. Division and subdivision had been carried to absurd lengths in an effort to avoid friction and improve tax-collection, in neither of which had it enjoyed any great success. Some attempt to provide greater cohesion was made in 1923–4, when Berber Province ceased to have any further say in Beja affairs, but the Atbai Besharin belonged to Red Sea Province, and the Atbara sections to Kassala, with the Hadendowa still split between the two, and it was not until the Kassala Cotton Company was given a concession to grow cotton in the Gash Delta in 1924–5 that the extent to which the administration of the Beja was out of hand was fully realized. The Hadendowa, ever since their arrival there at the end of the eighteenth century, had regarded the Gash as their particular preserve, a haven of water and grass when the rains elsewhere had failed. Moreover, it produced large quantities of excellent grain, the surplus of which was transported to the coast for export to the Hedjaz. It was therefore both a granary and a grazing area, and they viewed with the deepest suspicion and dislike the intrusion of a foreign company, with all the more reason because it was allowed to appropriate the best grain areas and to divert water from well-centres for cultivation of cotton, a crop in which they had then not the slightest interest.

In 1924 the area occupied by the company was about 9000 acres; by 1927 this had increased to 26,000, but despite this the scheme never prospered. The reasonable commercial demands of the company could not be made to square with the tribal rights of the Hadendowa, involving as they did loss of grain, grazing and water, and restriction of movement in their own territory. There was thus a fundamental clash of interests which could not be reconciled, and which gave rise to embittered relationships and a series of endless disputes in which the province authorities had the thankless task of attempting to hold the balance. The company, finding the Hadendowa uncooperative and unwilling to work, brought in cultivators from the Nile valley, and in so doing brought matters to a head. The Hadendowa, though refusing to take up cotton tenancies themselves, would not tolerate allocation of tribal land to strangers, and began a reign of terror against them which did not stop short of violence and murder.

Conditions grew steadily worse, so that the government was forced to intervene, and in 1929 took over the concession from the company, compensating it with land in the Gezira, and itself administering the scheme, as a commercial concern indeed, but one in which local rights and interests were given consideration to an extent which the company had not been able to do. Despite their poor record as cultivators 70% of the tenancies were allotted to Beja (mainly Hadendowa), and after over twenty years of politic administration by the Gash Board it can be said that the Beja have now no cause to regret the development of the cotton industry in the Gash, without which they would be an even poorer and more backward people than they are now. The Beja for their part have shown that while they can never be classed high as cultivators, they are not unadaptable to new conditions, and the whole scheme is worthy of study as a successful compromise between business and tribal interests. The extent to which Beja participation in the Gash scheme has increased since its inception is shown by the following tenancy tables:

	1926–7	1930–31	1950–51
Hadendowa	6,380	11,500	16,020
Other Beja	6,320	7,880	2,480
Non-Beja	8,410	7,410	5,120
Total	21,110	26,790	23,620

In the annual *Report on the Finances, Administration and Condition of the Sudan* for 1927 it was admitted with true official caution that 'the administration of the Beja-speaking tribes of the Eastern Sudan has long presented a problem to which no entirely satisfactory solution could be found'.[1] It was fully realized, however, that matters could not be allowed to continue thus, and as a first step a special commissioner for the Beja was appointed with authority throughout the whole Beja area irrespective of provincial boundaries, to study the problem, to make recommendations, and to put them into effect.[2] The result was the amalgamation of Red Sea Province with Kassala, the unification of the Hadendowa and of the Besharin, and the centralization of the administration of the bulk of the Beja tribes in District Headquarters at Sinkat. Taxation was simplified and reduced to collectable proportions, re-amalgamation of divided tribal units was encouraged, and under the new policy of native administration now being inaugurated a court system was set up in each tribe in which panels of local notables dealt with offences and civil cases by tribal custom.

The Hadendowa had long been ill-served by an ageing and unsatisfactory *naẓir*, and in 1927 he was replaced by Sheikh Mohammed Mohammed el Amin el Tirik, C.B.E., who from the very first gave evidence of those qualities of a tribal statesman and a leader of men which have been of such great value both to his tribe and to the government. The amalgamation of the Besharin under a single *naẓir* followed in 1929, and at the same time successful efforts were made to get rid of a crowd of useless and venial sheikhs and underlings. The system of annual tribal meetings by means of which so much of the administration of Beja is now carried on proved both effective and popular. Tribal confidence was restored, and for the next ten years or so the Beja prospered under a succession of sympathetic administrators who trekked extensively, got to know

[1] *Op. cit.* p. 10.
[2] This was Mr F. T. C. Young, later governor of Kassala and of Blue Nile Provinces. He was followed by Mr D. Newbold, later Sir Douglas Newbold, K.B.E., governor of Kordofan Province, and then Civil Secretary, Sudan Government.

and be known by the tribes, studied their customs and history, and, a few of them, achieved some degree of fluency in To Bedawie or Tigré. This is not to say that there were no set-backs: there were enough of these, but on the whole the period was one of consolidation and gradual progress, and Beja characteristics, which had once aroused fury and despair, were now looked upon more kindly as the foibles of a sturdy, independent and individualistic people, which could be tolerated and even admired.

Thus it was that when an Italian invasion of the Sudan was threatened during the summer and autumn of 1940, following the occupation of Kassala, the tribes which had once been designated as hostile, treacherous, or at the best indifferent, rallied to our support and (the Hadendowa in particular) rendered most valuable services. In the Tokar hills a small force of scouts, known as Meadowforce, kept watch against an Italian advance on Port Sudan which never came, and was finally disbanded in March 1941 after having taken part in the advance on Massawa. In the Gash a Hadendowa unit (Frosty-force) acted as scouts, intelligence agents, guides, and counter espionage corps. They were never, from a strictly orthodox military point of view, either a very smart or dependable force, but for the purposes for which they were employed there could have been none better, as the following extract from a captured Italian report eloquently bears witness:

After we took Kassala, and even today, no informer has been able to pass through the Hadendowa area. Any agent we send out fails to return.... Briefly, the English without troops kept an area secure between us and themselves by using the Hadendowa who are by nature thieves, brigands and warriors.[1]

With the defeat of the Italian forces in Eritrea the frontier area might have settled down quietly to a period of peace and rehabilitation had it not been that the said 'thieves and brigands' felt that they had been wrongly deprived of the spoils of victory.

[1] Sudan Government Archives.

They found themselves prevented from harrying and despoiling the Eritrean Beni Amer as they had had every intention of doing, and thus imbued with a sense of grievance and of the wrongness of things in general, the Gemilab section, the traditional guardians of the frontier area, and the least tractable of all the Hadendowa clans, began to raid Beni Amer settlements in Eritrea with the assistance and encouragement of the whole tribe, including even those responsible leaders who should have been foremost in restraining them. Their attitude being what it was, it proved all but impossible to bring the offenders to book, and the Beni Amer remained without the redress to which they were entitled. The result was that the Beni Amer too took the law into their own hands, and a number of armed bands, well equipped with rifles and ammunition which the Italians had either issued lavishly to native levies, or had abandoned in defeat, took to the more inaccessible hills, and began to counter-raid across the frontier with considerable effect.

For what was probably the first time in the long feud between the two tribes the Hadendowa got rather more than they gave, and found themselves at a hopeless disadvantage in opposing firearms with their traditional weapons of sword and spear. The Hadendowa have not yet outlived their distrust of the rifle as a weapon, and even when they possess them are inept in their use, and will abandon them after a shot or two in an attempt to rush in and use cold steel at close quarters. The Beni Amer raiding parties (known as *shifta*) had therefore little difficulty in disposing of such opposition as they encountered, and in a very short time had cleared the frontier, killing all Hadendowa whom they could find, driving off their herds, and from their winter bases in the Tokar hills making life unbearable for any Hadendowa in Khor Baraka and Khor Langeib, and as far south as Girgir, within a day's ride of Kassala.

The government, both in Eritrea and the Sudan, made lavish use of troops to suppress this banditry, in which others than the Hadendowa began to suffer as the *shifta* ran short of supplies, but with little success, their efforts resembling rather the use of a sledge hammer to crush a mosquito. The *shifta*, with a rifle strength of often not more than a dozen or fifteen men, could cover thirty miles in a night over country impossible for those unfamiliar with it or unable to travel extremely light. The troops, therefore, had very little chance of coming up with them, and the raiders were further assisted by the benevolent neutrality of the Sudan Beni Amer, who not only victualled and concealed them, but often joined them in major raids against the common enemy. For three years the situation showed little signs of improvement, but early in 1946 (for reasons which are still largely obscure) the *shifta* suddenly tired of the game and took advantage of an amnesty offered by the Eritrean authorities to surrender, and a series of peace meetings, involving compensation payments of several thousands of pounds took place between the two tribes.[1]

Apart from *shifta* troubles the period immediately following the war was one of general unrest among the Beni Amer both in Eritrea and the Sudan, when their Tigré sections for the first time began openly and actively to resist the dominance of their Nabtab overlords who, like the Scots nobility of the fifteenth and sixteenth centuries, had long been 'resolute champions of indefensible privileges'.[2] For this there were a number of reasons. Fifty years of administration by a government which imposed general peace and security had largely deprived the Nabtab of their role as protectors of their serf followers, and the disadvantages suffered by the latter were therefore no longer balanced by compensatory advantages. The Nabtab paid no tribute, but collected that of the Tigré with additional levies for themselves, and continued to require their services for milking and herding their cattle, and other menial tasks. Failing also to read the signs of the times they treated them still

---

[1] In 1948 inter-tribal war again unaccountably flared up along the frontier, with the *shifta* operating under a new set of leaders, and did not die down until 1951 as the result of energetic action by the authorities on both sides of the frontier.

[2] Buchan, *Montrose* (1928), p. 165.

PLATE V

(1) BENI AMER 'SHIFTA'

(2) POLICE PATROL IN THE RED SEA HILLS

as a people of inferior status with no assertable rights, and continued by all possible means to emphasize their caste superiority.

The war brought other trials for the serf peoples. There was a general shortage of supplies, and the Nabtab saw to it that the lion's share of any such commodities as cloth, coffee, grain and sugar went to themselves, and even when the Tigré, non-vocal and meek, got anything at all they had to pay the most exorbitant prices for it. The first rumblings of discontent were heard in 1944, and by 1947 there was open revolt. All efforts at a settlement acceptable to both sides having failed, at the beginning of 1948 the whole Beni Amer Nazirate was subjected to a complete social and administrative reorganization. The Nabtab were relegated to the position of a tribal section of equal status with any other, and the Tigré were organized in their ancient tribal groups, so that for the first time almost in centuries such names as the Almada, Wilinnoho, Asfada and others were once again in common use.

It is to be feared that after years of suppression the wine of freedom has gone rather to Tigré heads. They have few leaders of any calibre, and they suffer from the delusion that emancipation gives them licence to behave as they please without regard for administrative expediency or anything else, and they are inclined to feel frustrated that the nebulous Utopia of their own imagining has somehow evaded their grasp. The solution to their troubles lies in years of sympathetic but firm administration, and avoidance of fragmentation and tribal disruption. It may be that with the removal of the powerful cohesive tie of Nabtab domination the Beni Amer as a tribe will disintegrate and disappear, but it cannot be allowed to do so before some other administrative entity appears to take its place.

The administration of the Beja remains in all things tribal, and must so continue for as long as they are still predominantly nomadic. Only in Tokar, with its mixed breeds of townsmen and cultivators, has it been possible to experiment in local government on the model adopted elsewhere in the Sudan. The Tokar District Council, known locally as the *Meglis*

Ahli, was formally inaugurated in January 1948, and is now responsible for the administration of the town and delta, the Khor Baraka area, and the coastal strip of the Gwineb between the delta itself and Port Sudan. It consists of fifteen members elected by town, delta, and nomad wards, and eight members appointed by the governor, under the chairmanship of the district commissioner. From small beginnings it has continued to develop steadily, and its budget now balances at nearly £E. 25,000.

And here, without posing further problems of the future, it is fitting to take leave of the Beja, in summing up the efforts which have been made to improve his lot, and in estimating how far in fact such efforts have been successful. We have attempted to settle him in more productive areas, where he need no longer live, as in the Atbai, on the border-line of starvation: he declines resolutely to leave his inhospitable deserts. We have introduced him to the benefits of modern medical research: he prefers still his own more drastic remedies of knife and branding iron. We have provided him with schools and teachers to very little effect. We have developed to the best of our ability the few resources of his barren country in an effort to raise his standard of living and to stabilize his existence, but he prefers his remote mountain glen where he has to travel a dozen miles for a skinful of brackish water. He has perhaps learnt to tolerate and even like his rulers (or such of them as he sees), and to have some regard for the law and order which they impose, but he cannot be coerced beyond a certain point, and if he is, then swords come out and bloodshed follows. He remains, as ever, an independent fighting man, for whom the magnitude of the odds against him counts for little. If there were ever to be a Beja Thermopylae their three hundred would, I am sure, be capable of a characteristic gesture in true classical tradition:

the Spartans on the sea-wet rock sat down and combed their hair.

APPENDIX I

BEJA CHRONOLOGY

B.C.

c. 2750 Possible date of first exploitation of Eastern Desert gold mines by the VIth Dynasty.

c. 2650 Expedition to Punt sent out by Pepi II.

2000–1580 Middle Empire. Numerous expeditions to the Eastern Desert.

c. 1460 Hatepshut's expedition to Punt.

c. 1450 Exploitation of the Eastern Desert mines by the XVIIIth Dynasty.

c. 1330 Opening of the Derheib mine by Seti I, XIXth Dynasty.

1050 Mines abandoned after fall of XXth Dynasty.

c. 1000–600 Approximate date of Sabaean colonization of Tigrean highlands.

320–220 Exploitation of the Red Sea trade by the Ptolemies.

c. 290 Beja raided by Nastasenen of Meroë.

285 Ptolemais Theron (Agig) founded as an elephant depot.

275 Berenice founded by Ptolemy Philadelphus.

c. 110 Invasion of Africa by Abraha 'Dhu el Manar' from the Yemen.

40 Eastern Desert mines abandoned by the Ptolemies.

30 Roman occupation of Egypt.

23 Napata sacked by Roman expedition.

A.D.

47 Discovery of the monsoon by Hippalus.

52 Roman fleet sent to the Red Sea for suppression of piracy.

61 Nero's mission to Meroë.

64 Approximate date of *Periplus Maris Erythraei*, and first mention of Axum.

c. 90 Unsuccessful raid by Abu el Malik ibn Shamnar-Yerash on the Atbai.

137 Defeat of Beja in the Eastern Desert by Hadrian's generals.

241 Beja raid Upper Egypt.

268–75 Beja dominate Upper Egypt.

270 Aurelian negotiates with Axum.

275–82 Beja driven out by Probus.

284 Diocletian drew back the frontier and paid subsidies to prevent raiding.

c. 340 Axum converted to Christianity by Frumentius.

356 Aizanas of Axum destroys Meroë.

425–30 Beja raids on Egypt.

451 Beja subdued by Marcian's general, Maximinus.

525 Himyarite kingdom in the Yemen conquered by Asbaha of Axum.

533 Justin proposes anti-Persian alliance with Axum.

536 Temple of Isis at Philae closed by Justinian.

538–9 Repeated Beja raids on Upper Egypt.

540 Decisive defeat of the Beja by Silko of Nubia.

550–600 Nominal conversion of Beja to Christianity.

577 Last mention of Beja raids on Egypt.

c. 600 Appearance of Badi' as a Red Sea port. Bellou settlement in the Atbai.

641 Arab invasion of Egypt. Battle of Bahnasa.

690 Possible date of Halenga settlement in the Gash.

700–800 Decline of Axum.

800 Approximate date of Arteiga settlement at Suakin.

831 Expedition against the Beja under Abdullah ibn Jiham.

854 Rising of the Beja, who raided as far as Esna.

855 Defeat of Beja by Mohammed Abdullah ibn Gami'.

878 Re-opening of Wadi Allagi mines by Abu Ommari Abdel Rahman.

900 Approximate date of Yagoubi's description of six Beja kingdoms between Assuan and Dahlak.

945 Rabi'a at the height of their power in the Eastern Desert mines.

969 Destructive raid on Upper Egypt by Beja.

1028 First mention of Aidhab as a pilgrim port.

c. 1150 Badi' abandoned by its inhabitants.

1183 Aidhab sacked by the Crusaders.

1266 Mamluke expedition against Suakin.

1270 Approximate date of Kawahla settlement in the Atbai.

1326 Aidhab visited by Ibn Batuta.

1341 Eastern Desert mines exhausted and abandoned.

1422 First Indian cargo ship berthed at Suakin.

1426 Aidhab destroyed by Bars Bey.

c. 1470 Hadareb (Bellou) driven from the Atbai by Besharin.

1490 Mission of Pedro de Covilham to Abyssinia.

1500–1600 Infiltration of Northern Tigré by Bellou and other Beja.

1504 Foundation of the Fung kingdom by Omara Dunkas.

1520 Occupation of Suakin and Massawa by Ottoman Turks.

1520–50 Expulsion of Bellou from Sinkat area by Hadendowa.

c. 1530 Invasion of Red Sea coast by Beit Asgadé (Habab).

1580 Overthrow of the Bellou by the Nabtab (Beni Amer).

c. 1720 Beginning of western expansion of the Amarar.

c. 1750 Besharin migration to the Atbara.

1800 Hadendowa in occupation of the Gash and middle Atbara.

1814 Burckhardt visited Taka and Suakin.

1821 Egyptian occupation of the Sudan.

1823 First Egyptian raid on Taka under the Defterdar.

1832, 1836 Further raids by Khurshid Pasha.

1833 Linant de Bellefonds visits the Atbai.

1840 Town of Kassala founded by the Egyptians.

1844 Expedition to Taka by Ahmed Pasha Menekli.

1848 Egyptian agreement with the Beni Amer.

1864 Mutiny of the 4th Regiment at Kassala.

1872 Munziger occupies Keren.

1875 Battle of Gundet. Egyptian defeat by Abyssinians.

1876 Battle of Gura. Another Egyptian defeat.

1881 Outbreak of the Mahdia.

1883 Unsuccessful attack on Sinkat by Osman Digna. First battle of El Teb.

1884 Second (Baker's) battle of El Teb. Fall of Sinkat and Tokar. Third (Graham's) battle of El Teb. Battle of Tamai.

1885 Fall of Khartoum. Battle of Tofrik (McNeill's Zeriba).

1888 Battle of Gimmeiza.

1891 Re-occupation of Tokar.

1894 Italians captured Kassala.

1897 Kassala re-occupied on transfer from Italians.

1898 Battle of Omdurman.

1900 Capture of Osman Digna.

1918 The Sambo Incident. Attack on Kassala fort by Hadendowa.

1924 Inception of cotton growing in the Gash by the Kassala Cotton Company.

APPENDIX I

1928 Unification of Beja administration under Kassala Province.
1929 Gash Board took over from Kassala Cotton Company.
1939–40 Italian occupation of Kassala.
1943–6 Beni Amer-Hadendowa frontier troubles
1948 Emancipation of Beni Amer serfs. Inauguration of Tokar
    District Council.

APPENDIX II

BEJA TRIBES AND SUB-DIVISIONS

Beja District

(1) AMARAR   67,000

They are divided into two main groups, the Amarar proper, and the Otman. Of the former are the:

Fadlab	Esheibab

The Otman are divided into:

Aliab:	Arfoiab	Keilab
	Manfolab	Minniab
Gwilai:	Musiab	Omar Hassaiab
	Sindereit	Abdel Rahimab
	Abdel Rahmanab	
Kurbab		
Nurab (in Tokar District)		

(2) BESHARIN   45,000

They are divided as follows:

Um Ali:	Aliab	Amrab
	Hamadorab	Shinterab
Um Nagi:	Eiraiab	Wailaliab
	Nafi'ab	Batran
	Mansurab	Madakir
	Adloiab	Mashbolab
	Hammadab	Garab

Of the Um Nagi the first four sections are in the Atbai, the remainder on the river Atbara.

(3) HADENDOWA   110,000

Their most important sections are:

Wailaliab	Bushariab
Samarar	Meishab
Gemilab	Shara'ab
Hakolab	Samarandowab

(3) HADENDOWA (*continued*)

Ger'ib	Tirik
Kalolai	Emirab
Hamdab	Shaboidinab
Beiranab	Gurhabab
Buglinai	Rabamak

(4) KAMMALAB and MORGHUMAB   1,200

(5) SIGOLAB and MELHITKINAB   800

                                                   Total   224,000

Tokar District

(6) BENI AMER   30,000

They are divided as follows:

Nabtab
Egeilab

Tigré:	Almada	Meikal
	Asfada	Aflanda
	Targeila	Wilinnoho
	Hamasein	Ad Fadil
	Abhasheila	Rigbat
Hadareb:	Sinkatkinab	Beit Musa
	Labat	Sogaiet
	Hadoigoboiab	Beit Awat
	Libis	Beit Goreish
	Ad Kokoi	Ad el Khasa

(7) ARTEIGA   4,000

(8) SHAIAB   3,500

(9) ASHRAF   2,500

(10) KIMMEILAB   2,000

(11) HASSANAB   1,000

                                                   Total   43,000

Kassala District

(12) BENI AMER   15,000
                    Subdivided as above

(13) HALENGA   2,500

                                                   Total   17,500

APPENDIX II

Gedaref District

(14) HAMRAN   700

SUMMARY

Beja District	224,000
Tokar District	43,000
Kassala District	17,500
Gedaref District	700
Grand total	285,200

APPENDIX III

THE ARTEIGA TRIBES

The Arteiga claim to be descended from the Ashraf, and more particularly from Mohammed Gamal el Din, one of the sons of Ba Saffar, who is said to have migrated from the Hadramaut to Suakin about A.D. 800. A race of traders, they extended their influence by marriage with Beja tribes such as the Boikinab and Bellou, and latterly with Amarar and Besharin; and in contemporary legend Ba Saffar is described as a pearl-fisher and merchant whose stock-in-trade consisted mainly of pearls and slave-girls. Being among the very earliest of the post-Islamic settlers they managed to gain a position among the Beja never attained by later immigrants. A politic, ambitious and resourceful people, they secured their position by marriage with local women to an extent which others did not care or were not permitted to do.

When the Bellou were pushed south at the turn of the sixteenth century the Arteiga replaced them as the masters of Suakin, and inherited also from them the old Beja name of Hadareb or Hadarba, by which they became known all over the Sudan. The emir of the Hadarba, who shared the pickings of the port with the Turco-Egyptian governors, was also the chief of the Arteiga, and lived on the mainland with his people who organized trade in slaves and other goods with the interior, and who are remarked on with little favour by Burckhardt at Shendi and elsewhere in 1813. In the course of their trade they established relations also with Messellemia in the Gezira, famous, like Shendi, as a slave market. 'À Suakin vivent les Hadarbé, grands voyageurs qui ont un succursale à Messalamié. . . . Ils forment une race peu nombreuse, mais influent par son aisance, son intelligence et son aptitude à s'assimiler les progrès apportés par les Européens.'[1]

The Shanabla who lived in the Gezira between Wadi Medani and Hasaheisa, and who are not to be confused with the nomad Shanabla of Kordofan, account themselves Kawahla, and say that they result from the union of Kimmeilab with Hadareb or Hudur wives from Arbagi, a once prosperous town on the Blue Nile destroyed by the

[1] Douin, *Histoire du Regne du Khedive Ismail*, vol. III (1936), pt. I, p. 31.

Shukria in about 1784, and they remain to this day an aristocratic family group rather than a tribe.

The main body of the Arteiga moved from Suakin to Tokar about the beginning of the nineteenth century, and were the first to cultivate in the Delta, on payment of dues to the Beni Amer, who used it as a grazing ground only. With the introduction of cotton their fortunes were made, and they are today very well-to-do, at least by local standards. They are a clever and unscrupulous people, their town-dwelling sections much given to dissipation, who have exploited their position as the largest allotment holders in Tokar Delta with no less business acumen than they once did their control of the lucrative Suakin trade routes.[1] They are now divided into three well-defined groups, a small but aristocratic remnant in Suakin, the main body in Tokar, and an offshoot of the latter in the Gash, where they are now under the Hadendowa Nazirate.

The Shaiab, who are accounted a branch of the Arteiga, are now tribally distinct. Whereas the Arteiga are mainly town-dwellers, merchants and cultivators, the Shaiab are nomad cattle- and camel-owners, a wild, unruly, truculent tribe, in all respects true Beja, and little distinguishable from the common type of Red Sea nomad. They are concentrated mainly on the fringes of Tokar Delta, to which however, they are late-comers, and are to be found also in the Gash and Khor Arbaat, and scattered thinly along the coast between Port Sudan and Suakin. They have land holdings in Tokar Delta, but are indifferent cultivators, even by Beja standards, and are still mainly interested in their herds.

The relationship of the Hamran to the Arteiga is less easily traceable than that of the Shaiab, and they themselves like to consider that they are of pure Arab stock, and a branch of the Harb. It is more generally accepted, however, that they derive from the Arteiga, their ancestor being one Mohammed Aderob (the Red) who migrated first to the Atbara and thence to the Setit where they now are. Here they intermarried with the local tribes, and acquired fame as hunters of elephant and other game by the methods described so graphically by Baker. They were in those days a powerful clan (Myres in 1874 mentions numerous Hamran villages) and in the

[1] Cameron, writing in 1886, speaks of 'the savage Artegas' and classes them with the Hadendowa as the tribes most hostile to the government ('On the Tribes of the Eastern Sudan', *J.R.A.S.* No. 16 (1886), p. 291).

Mahdia they remained loyal to the government and helped to victual Kassala. For this they were harried and all but exterminated by the Dervishes, and now number not more than a few hundreds inhabiting two or three villages on the Setit.

It is not impossible also that the Gharasia/Hamar of Kordofan are similarly derived, as they allege that they are descended from a Himyarite tribe which crossed the Red Sea at the end of the seventh century (a date rather too early for the Arteiga) and settled for a time near Taka. It is of interest too that of the Beni Fadl (a tribe of Jaaliin origins related to the Manasir and Rubatab, but now merged with the Hamar) one section is called Hadarma (Hadarba) and another Hamran. The connection with the East is denied, but the naming of these sub-sections is probably more than pure coincidence. Certain sections of the Hadendowa, some of the Kalolai, and the Erhai/Gaidab claim a Hamran ancestry, so that by and large the blood of Mohammed the Red has been very widely diffused.

The probability that the Hamran are Arteiga is strengthened by the fact that like them they adhere to the Shafi' cult, the only other tribe in the Sudan to do so other than a few Ashraf in Khor Baraka. They were also, like the Halenga, until fairly recently a Tigré-speaking people. Baker describes his hunting companions as 'agagir', the Tigré word for hunters, but whereas the Halenga with their northern Beja contacts have abandoned Tigré for To Bedawie, the Hamran (now part of the Shukria Nazirate) like to pretend that they have never spoken anything but Arabic.

The relationship of the three tribes is best illustrated by a genealogical tree:

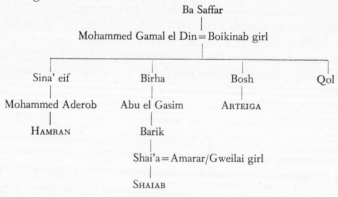

APPENDIX IV

THE ABABDA

They themselves claim a Kawahla descent from Zubeir ibn Awam who was killed at the 'Battle of the Camel', as follows:

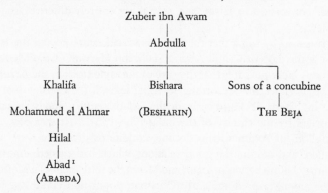

Zubeir ibn Awam

Abdulla

Khalifa — Bishara — Sons of a concubine

Mohammed el Ahmar — (BESHARIN) — THE BEJA

Hilal

Abad [1]
(ABABDA)

There are many authorities, however, who would dispute this, in favour of a Hamitic origin, or at least a large preponderance of Beja blood. I myself prefer to believe the tribal legends which allege that they came to Egypt in the army of 'Amr ibn el 'Asi and occupied the Nile valley south of Assuan shortly after the battle of Bahnasa (641). There they intermarried with the local Berberine (Kunuz) population, and also with their Beja neighbours in the Eastern Desert, so that today they are a mongrel people of mixed blood, some of whose nomadic sections in Egypt speak a dialect of To Bedawie.

Other sections, those who pushed south into the Sudan, and are now to be found in the Northern Province in Berber and Shendi Districts, would certainly claim to be pure Arabs, and appear to have no Beja characteristics or affinities. An adaptable race, with a reputation for close-fistedness, they are excellent guides and camel masters, and it is alleged that the Fung used to employ them to guard caravans over the desert routes from Korosko to Abu Hamed.

[1] The name is also said to be derived from 'Abad = a desert in the Berberine dialect of the Kunuz, or from 'Abād = Christian Arabs.

THE HALENGA

This small tribe, now only about 2500 strong, is of interest as being probably the first of the Ishmaelite Arabs to enter the Sudan after conversion to Islam, and by a route entirely different to any others.

It is said by some that they are Beni Saad, who crossed the Red Sea in the days of Caliph Abu el Malik ibn Marwan (A.D. 685–705) but it is more probable that they are of the same stock as the Arabian tribe of Hawazin. According to tribal legend, they settled first in the highlands of Tigré early in the eighth century and were later expelled by the enmity of the indigenous tribes. At that time the kingdom of Axum was in decline, conditions generally were unsettled, and despite the good relations which had existed almost a century before between Axum and Mecca the settlement of a Moslem tribe among a predominantly Christian population could not but have led to discord.

The Halenga, thus ousted, fled by way of the valley of the Mareb (Gash) until they came to Taka, where they settled in the vicinity of the great hill of To Lus (Jebal Kassala) and extended their authority and cultivations as far north as Deba'ab (Mekali) in the Gash Delta and beyond. Here they intermarried not only with local Beja and Tigré tribes (Beni Amer, Gadein, Bilein, Haffara, Sigolab, Melhitkinab and others) but also with Arabs such as the Abdullab, Ashraf, Rubatab, and Jaaliin, a process which still continues. They are connected also with the Khawawid who are to be found in the vicinity of Kabushia in the Northern Province. Legend relates that at some date unknown a Halengi holy man settled at Abu Tleih on the fringes of the Bayuda Desert (later the site of the Desert Column's battle in 1885) and there married a girl of the local tribe of Awadia. Deciding later to rejoin his own people with his wife he got no farther than Kabushia on the east bank of the Nile, because in crossing the river she gave birth to a son who was therefore nicknamed El Khawwad (the Wader).

There is an interesting reference to the Halenga in the manuscript of Sheikh Ahmed el Fiki el Ma'aref:

PLATE VI

JEBAL KASSALA

It is said that beyond the strong places of Taka and between them and Ethiopia is a great mountain called El Lus where the Companions of the Cave are believed to be: and those who live in these strong places are called Halanka.[1]

In about 1780 the Fung sultan, Adlan II, sent an expedition against them which was unsuccessful, both its leaders being killed.

In the late eighteenth century the Hadendowa, pressing southwards to the Atbara, drove them in on Jebal Kassala and their main settlement of Fakenda, roughly on the same site as the present-day town of Kassala, and they were later to earn enduring ill-fame among the Beja by calling in the Egyptians in the hope of redressing their fortunes. The result was the plundering expeditions of Ahmed Pasha Abu 'Udan and Ahmed Pasha el Menekli and the founding of Kassala, and though it is true that for a short time the Halenga enjoyed some prosperity as minor officials and auxiliaries under Turco-Egyptian rule, they paid for it in the Mahdia when they were all but exterminated.

Lejean, who visited Kassala in 1860, believed, erroneously, from their language and customs that they were a tribe of the Hamasein, and remarks that they are the only Tigré-speaking tribe whose social system gives equality to all. Werne, who accompanied Ahmed Pasha Abu 'Udan's expedition in 1840, gives them grudging praise as 'in general a fine race; they have open countenances in which is not visible that savageness and falseness so marked in those of the Haddenda, although, in truth, there is little to choose between them'.[2]

They are today predominantly of mixed Arab strain with a dash of Tigré blood, and a lesser one of other Beja. Nevertheless, To Bedawie has now replaced Tigré as their mother tongue, though many are trilingual, speaking Arabic and Tigré as well. They are to be found mainly in Kassala town and its environs, though legend has it that some of the sections of the Aliab/Amarar have Halenga blood in their veins. Though now tribally weak and insignificant, they are a quick-witted, handsome, and adaptable people whose mongrel breeding has not yet affected their tribal consciousness.

[1] Macmichael, *A History of the Arabs in the Sudan* (1922), vol. II, p. 348.
[2] Werne, *African Wanderings* (1852), p. 185.

APPENDIX VI

THE FELLATA MELLE

An interesting and very recent example of assimilation of Beja customs and habits by a non-Beja tribe is afforded by the Fellata Melle, a small group consisting of about half a dozen encampments, which lives near Gulusit, a few miles north of Kassala, where there is also a very large community of other West Africans, Hausa, Bornu, etc.

The original group emigrated from Timbuctoo about 1901–2 on the pilgrimage to Mecca, and on its return settled on the west side of the Gash Delta at Gulusit. Since then they have increased considerably in numbers and wealth, acquired herds of cattle and goats, and a few camels, and have re-adopted a semi-nomadic way of life. Like other nomads of the Eastern Sudan they live in tents of fibre or grass matting, but in shape similar to the beehive dwellings of the sedentary West African.

What, however, is much more remarkable, is their adoption of the Beja language, weapons, way of dressing, etc. so that the younger generation with its mop of hair and scratching pins, flowing garments and loose, baggy trousers, characteristic curved dagger and shoulder-slung sword and shield are, at first sight, indistinguishable from the Hadendowa among whom they live, and to whose administration they belong.

APPENDIX VII

THE BEJA CAMEL

The camel appears to have become known in Egypt about 550 B.C., and to have been used for desert transport work both by the Ptolemies and the Romans, though never in any great numbers. When the Beja first acquired it, and began to breed the herds which have since contributed not a little to the aridity of their deserts, is not known, but by the third century A.D. when they first began to trouble the Romans in Egypt they had not only acquired great numbers of them, but had also become extremely skilled in riding and managing them. It is an art which they have not lost. Medieval observers have remarked on their ability to handle their cumbrous mounts in battle as easily as horses, and I have myself at tribal gatherings witnessed feats of great dexterity—riders who stood upright in the saddle guiding their camels with one hand while brandishing a naked sword in the other, or who carried a bowl of milk, riding at full tilt, without spilling a drop.

The breeding of pedigree strains is confined to a few of the northern sections of the Besharin and Amarar, most famous of which are the Ba Nagir and Kiliewau bred by the Hamadorab and Aliab Besharin respectively. The much-prized Kiliewau are in origin a cross between Ba Nagir and Abidiya strains (the sire being of the former) but has now come to be bred exclusively by the Aliab as the result of constant crossing with Aliab dams.

The Beshari camels of the Atbai are probably the finest to be found in the Sudan, strong, well-shaped beasts, bred for endurance and pace, and admirably suited for patrol work and travel in the desert.[1]

The Kurbab section of the Amarar also breed an extremely good type of what might be called an 'all-purpose' camel. They are extremely hardy and well-paced, but incline to be small, and are therefore less useful as weight carriers.

Only a few of the Hadendowa sections breed camels and none of any great distinction.

[1] Beshari camels can usually maintain a comfortable riding pace of about 5 m.p.h. as a maximum. At greater speeds they cease to be comfortable.

The Beni Amer, even more than the Hadendowa, are a cattle-owning tribe, but the Nabtab introduced camels into the hill area south of Khor Baraka some 350 years ago, and one section, the Barhamai, have since bred a distinctive hill type, rather leggy and far from comfortable to ride, but sure-footed and dependable over country which a plains-bred camel would not face.

Camels which are bred under desert conditions rarely do well in more fertile areas and vice versa, and nearly all find difficulty in adapting themselves to different types of grazing. This is particularly so of camels bred in Tokar District (mainly by Shaiab and Nurab) where they are grazed almost exclusively on the saltbush which flourishes on the coast and in Khor Baraka, deprived of which they lose condition very rapidly and often decline past recovery. For this reason Tokar-bred camels have almost no market outside the district.

BIBLIOGRAPHY

An asterisk indicates titles reprinted or published by Frank Cass, London.

CHAPTER I

For a short description of the Beja there is nothing to compare with 'The Beja Tribes of the Red Sea Hills', by D. Newbold, to be found in *The Anglo-Egyptian Sudan from Within*, ed. by J. A. de C. Hamilton (London, 1935).

CHAPTER II

There is no special bibliography for this chapter, but those who are interested in further study of the Beja should consult the following articles in *Sudan Notes and Records*:

SANDARS. 'The Besharin', vol. XVI (2) (1933).
SANDARS. 'The Amarar', vol. XVIII (2) (1935).
OWEN. 'The Hadendowa', vol. XX (2) (1937).
CLARK. 'The Manners, Customs and Beliefs of the Northern Beja', vol. XXI (1) (1938).
PAUL. 'Notes on the Beni Amer', vol. XXXI (2) (1950).

CHAPTER III

CAMERON. 'On the Tribes of the Eastern Sudan', *J.R.A.S.* No. 16 (1887).
CROWFOOT. 'Some Lacunae in the Anthropology of the Anglo-Egyptian Sudan', *J.B.A.* (1907).
ELLIOT SMITH. *The Ancient Egyptians* (New York, 1911).
KEANE. 'The Ethnology of the Egyptian Sudan', *J.R.A.I.* vol. XIV (1885).
MURRAY. 'The Northern Beja', *J.R.A.S.* No. 57 (1927).
PALMER. 'Observations from Mr Francis Rodd's Rock Drawings from Air compared with Dr Winkler's Rock Drawings from the Eastern Desert of Upper Egypt', *Man*, No. 106 (1939).
SELIGMAN. 'Some Aspects of the Hamitic Problem in the Anglo-Egyptian Sudan', *J.R.A.S.* No. 43 (1913). 'Notes on the Besharin', *Man*, No. 47 (1915).
WINKLER. *Rock Drawings of Southern Upper Egypt*, vol. I (Oxford, 1938).

CHAPTER IV

A. DYNASTIC

BLOSS. 'Relics of Ancient Gold Mines', *S.N.R.* vol. XX (2) (1937).
CHABAS. *Inscriptions des Mines d'Or* (Paris, 1862).
DUNN. *Notes on the Mineral Deposits of the Anglo-Egyptian Sudan* (Cairo, 1911).
HAMY. 'Les Pays des Troglodytes', *L'Anthropologie*, vol. II (1897).
* MACMICHAEL. *A History of the Arabs in the Sudan*, vol. I (Cambridge, 1922).
NEWBOLD. 'Deraheib Gold Mines', *Antiquity*, No. 22 (1948).

BIBLIOGRAPHY

B. PTOLEMAIC

BEVAN. *A History of Egypt under the Ptolemaic Dynasty* (London, 1927).
DIODORUS SICULUS. *Bibliothicae Historicae Libri qui Supersunt* (Amsterdam, 1746).
MAHAFFY. *History of Egypt under the Ptolemaic Dynasty* (London, 1894).
ROSTOVTZEFF. 'Ptolemaic Egypt', *Cambridge Ancient History*, vol. VII (1928).

CHAPTER V

BENT. *The Sacred City of the Ethiopians* (London, 1896).
BUDGE. *A History of Ethiopia, Nubia, and Abyssinia*, vols. I, II (London, 1928).
BUXTON. *Travels in Ethiopia* (London, 1949).
KAMMERER. *Essaie sur l'Histoire antique d'Abyssinie, le Royaume d'Axum et le voisin d'Arabie et de Meroë* (Paris, 1926).
McCRINDLE (Ed.). *The Christian Topography of Cosmas* (London, Hakluyt Society, 1897).
SALT. *A Voyage to Abyssinia, 1809–10* (London, 1814).
SCHOFF (Ed.). *The Periplus of the Erythrean Sea* (New York, 1912).
VALENTIA. *Voyages and Travels to India, Ceylon, the Red Sea and Abyssinia 1802–06*, vol. III (London, 1809).

CHAPTER VI

BUDGE. *A History of Ethiopia, etc.* vol. I (London, 1928).
BUTLER. *The Arab Conquest of Egypt and the Last Thirty Years of Roman Domination* (Oxford, 1902).
CAUSSIN DE PERCIVAL. *Essaie sur l'Histoire des Arabes avant l'Islamisme*, vol. I (Paris, 1847–48).
CROWFOOT. 'The Island of Meroë', *Archaeological Survey of Egypt* (London, 1911).
KIRWAN. *Oxford University Excavations at Firka*, App. III (Oxford, 1939).
KIRWAN. 'A Survey of Nubian Origins', *S.N.R.* vol. XX (1) (1937).
KIRWAN. 'A Contemporary Account of the Conversion of the Sudan to Christianity', *S.N.R.* vol. XX (2) (1937).
KIRWAN. 'Studies in the Later History of Nubia', *Liverpool Annals*, No. 24.
* MACMICHAEL. *A History of the Arabs in the Sudan*, vol. I (Cambridge, 1922).
MILNE. *A History of Egypt under Roman Rule.* Rev. ed. (London, 1924).
MOMSEN. *The Provinces of the Roman Empire*, vol. II (London, 1909).
PROCOPIUS. *De Bello Persico.*
REVILLOUT. *Mémoirs sur les Blemmyes* (Mémoire presentée à l'Academie des Inscriptions et Belle Lettres. No. 17. Paris, 1874).
STRABO. *Rerum Geographicarum*, Book XVII, 1, 2.
VAN DYKE. *A History of the Arabs and their Literature* (Cairo, 1893).
WINKLER. *Rock Drawings of Southern Upper Egypt* (Oxford, 1938).
WOOLLEY AND McIVER. *Karanog: The Romano-Nubian Cemetery* (Philadelphia, 1910).
WOOLLEY. *Karanog: The Town* (Philadelphia, 1911).

BIBLIOGRAPHY

CHAPTER VII

Bloss. 'The Story of Suakin', *S.N.R.* vol. xix (1) (1936), xx (2) (1937).

Burckhardt. *Travels in Nubia.* 2nd ed. App. iii (London, 1822).

Floyer. *Études sur le Nord Etbai* (Cairo, 1893).

Hebbert. 'El Rih—A Red Sea Island', *S.N.R.* vol. xviii (2) (1935).

Hobson. 'Chinese Porcelain Fragments from Aidhab', *Trans. of the Oriental Ceramic Society*, 1926/27.

Ibn Batuta (d. 1368). *Travels in Asia and Africa.* Broadway Travellers Series (London, 1929).

Ibn Khaldun (d. 1406). *El 'Ibar wa Diwan el Mutabda wa el Khabar,* (Bulac, 1867).

* Lane-Poole. *A History of Egypt in the Middle Ages* (London, 1901).

* Macmichael. *A History of the Arabs in the Sudan,* vol. i (Cambridge, 1922).

Makrizi (d. 1422). *El Khitat wa el Athar.*

Masudi (d. 956). *Muruj el Dhahab.* (Also French trans. *Les Prairies d'Or,* Mesnard and Courteille, vol. iii, Paris, 1861).

Murray. *The Sons of Ishmael* (London, 1935).

Newbold. 'The Crusaders in the Red Sea and the Sudan', *S.N.R.* vol. xxvi (2) (1945).

Qalqashandi (d. 1418). *Sobh el Asha* (Cairo, 1913).

Quatremere. *Mémoires Géographiques et Histoiriques sur l'Egypte,* vol. ii (Paris, 1811).

Sandars and Owen. 'Note on Ancient Villages in Khor Nubt and Khor Omek', *S.N.R.* vol. xxxii (2) (1951).

Yagoubi (d. 893). *Kitab el Buldan.*

CHAPTER VIII

Crowfoot. 'Some Red Sea Ports of the Anglo-Egyptian Sudan, *J.R.G.S.* No. 37 (1911).

Longrigg. *A Short History of Eritrea* (Oxford, 1945).

Munziger. *Ostafricanische Studien* (Schaffhausen, 1864).

Nadel. 'Notes on Beni Amer Society', *S.N.R.* vol. xxvi (1) (1945).

Paul. 'Notes on the Beni Amer', *S.N.R.* vol. xxxi (2) (1950).

Rossini. *Studi su Populazione dell Etiopia* (Rome, 1914).

Seligman. 'Past History and Present Condition of the Beni Amer', *S.N.R.* vol. xii (2) (1930).

Wyche. *A Short Relation of the River Nile* (London, 1673).

CHAPTER IX

Browne. *The History and Description of Africa of Leo Africanus, done into English by John Pory 1600* (London, Hakluyt Society, 1896), vol. iii.

Burckhardt. *Travels in Nubia.* 2nd. ed. (London, 1822).

Cumming. 'The History of Kassala and the Province of Taka', *S.N.R.* vol. xx (1) (1937), xxiii (2) (1940).

de Bellefonds. *L'Etbaye* (Paris, 1884).

Douin. *Histoire du Regne du Khedive Ismail,* vol. iii, pts. 1 and 2 (Cairo, 1936).

BIBLIOGRAPHY

JUNKER. *Travels in Africa, 1875–78* (London, 1890).
KENNEDY COOKE. 'The Red Sea Coast in 1540', *S.N.R.* vol. XVI (2) (1933).
LEJEAN. *Voyage au Deux Nils* (Paris, 1862).
LUCAS. 'On the Natives of Suakin and the Besharin Vocabulary', *J.R.A.I.* (1876).
PARRY. 'Narrative of an Expedition from Suakin to the Soudan, completed from the Journal of the late Capt. Langham Rokeby R. M.', *J.R.G.S.* No. 44 (1871).
SCHWEINFURTH. *Das Land am Elba und Sotriba Gibirge* (Berlin, 1885).
WERNE. *Africa Wanderings* (London, 1852).

CHAPTER X

CROMER. *Modern Egypt*, vols. I, II (London, 1908).
DE COSSON. *Days and Nights of Service* (London, 1886).
GLEICHEN. *The Anglo-Egyptian Sudan*, vol. I (London, 1905).
HILL. 'The Suakin-Berber Railway', *S.N.R.* vol. XX (1937).
JACKSON. *Osman Digna* (London, 1926).
ROYLE. *The Egyptian Campaign—1882–85.* Rev. ed. (London, 1902).
SARTORIOUS. *Three Months in the Sudan* (London, 1885).
THEOBALD. *The Mahdia* (London, 1951).
∗ WINGATE. *Mahdiism in the Egyptian Sudan* (London, 1891). *Report on the Dervish Rule in the Eastern Sudan* (Sudan Government Archives) (1891).

GENERAL

HAMILTON (Ed.). *The Anglo-Egyptian Sudan from Within* (London, 1935).
ROBINSON. 'Desiccation or destruction', *S.N.R.* vol. XVIII (1) (1935).
WRIGHT. *Geographical Lore at the Time of the Crusades* (New York, 1925).

APPENDIX III

BURCKHARDT. *Travels in Nubia.* 2nd ed. (London, 1822).
JACKSON. *Osman Digna* (London, 1926).
∗ MACMICHAEL. *A History of the Arabs in the Sudan*, vol. II, pt. III. (Cambridge, 1922).
MYERS. *Life with the Hamran Arabs* (London, 1876).
BAKER. *The Nile Tributaries of Abyssinia and the Sword Hunters of the Hamran Arabs* (London, 1908).
   The two latter works, despite their titles, are records of hunting trips, and concerned mainly with big game and shooting adventures.

APPENDIX V

HAMILTON. 'The Halenga', *S.N.R.* vol. VIII (1925).
LEJEAN. *Voyage au Deux Nils* (Paris, 1862).
∗ MACMICHAEL. *A History of the Arabs in the Sudan*, vol. II (Cambridge, 1922).
WERNE. *African Wanderings* (London, 1852).

APPENDIX VI

HAMILTON. 'Notes on the Fellata Melle of Kassala', *S.N.R.* vol. IX (1) (1926)

GLOSSARY

Badana: division of a tribe.

Diglel: title of chief of the Beni Amer.

Hissa: sub-division of a tribe.

Jebal: mountain, hill.

Khor: watercourse, dry except in the
    rainy season.

Mangil: a Fung title.

Mudir: governor.

Nazir: paramount chief of a tribe.

Wadi: valley, large watercourse.

INDEX

INDEX

Memphis, 29
Menelaeus, 31
Merefab, 25
Meroë, 31, 43, 45, 51, 133; Island of,
54 n.
Meroitic Empire, 54
Mersa Sha'ab, 12
Messellemia (tribe), 96; (town), 140
Middle Ages, 28
Middle East, 66
Middle Empire, 28, 133
Milne, 48 n.
Min, 60 n.
Minniab (Amarar), 137
Mithras, 60 n.
Mohammed, the Prophet, 44, 50, 51
Mohammed Abdullah ibn Gami', 68,
69, 71, 134
Mohammed Aderob (the Red), 141,
142
Mohammed Agim, 96
Mohammed Ahmed el Mahdi, 106,
107, 108, 110, 112
Mohammed Ali the Great, 91, 98, 99,
103
Mohammed Bey, the Defterdar, 99,
135
Mohammed Din, 100
Mohammed Gamal el Din, 140, 142
Mohammed Ghol (port of), 115, 122
Mohammed Hadab, 77
Mohammed Hassan ibn Kala'oun, 76
Mohammed Idris Adara, 82, 83
Mohammed Mohammed el Amin el
Tirik, 127
Mohammed Mubarak, the Fearless,
77
Mohammedans, 37
Mommsen, 59
Monsoon, 133
Monumentum Adulitanum, 33, 43,
51
Morghumab, 96, 138
Moslems, 37, 64, 67, 68, 70, 72
Mosophagi, 36
Mudr, 72
Mu'izz, 64 n., 72

Munziger, 65 n., 66, 101, 102, 104,
105, 135
Murray, 21, 79
Musiab (Amarar), 137
Musmar, 68 n., 96
Myres, 141

Nabtab, 17, 82, 84, 85, 86, 87, 88, 102,
130, 131, 135, 138, 148
Nafi'ab (Besharin), 137
Naga el Deir, 22
Nagash, 69, 71
Napata, 41, 52, 92, 133
Nasir ibn Kala'oun, 75
Nastasenen, 31, 133
Negran, 82
Nero, 133
Newbold, Sir Douglas, 2 n., 28 n.,
74 n., 124 n., 127 n.
Newbolt, 111 n.
New Empire, 28
Nile, R., 12, 20, 27, 29, 30, 31, 32 n.,
33, 41, 42, 45, 52, 54, 55, 58, 62,
68, 70, 71, 92
Nonnus, 48
Northern Province, 143, 144
Nuba, 3, 24, 35, 46, 52, 56, 57, 60, 61,
63
Nubia, 28, 62, 67, 75, 91; Lower
Nubia, 20
Nubian forest, 32
Nubians, Middle Group C, 22
Nubt, 68 n.
Nurab (Amarar), 16, 96, 114, 137, 148

Odi, 12, 15, 97
Odyssey, 30 n.
Olbab, 68, 69
Olympiodorus, 54 n., 59
Omara Dunkas, 77, 135
Omar (Caliph), 72
Omar Hassaiab (Amarar), 137
Ombi, 33
Omdurman, battle of, 117, 118, 135
Ommayads, 75
Oryx, 20 n.
Osiris, 37 n.

INDEX